SPIRITUAL *Discovery* SERIES

RECOVERY FOR
co·de·pen·den·cy

STEVEN E. STILES

Radiant Life

1445 Boonville Avenue   Springfield, MO 65802-1894
02-0122

STAFF

National Director: LeRoy R. Bartel
Editor in Chief: Michael H. Clarensau
Series Editor: Clancy Hayes
Assistant Editors: Lori Van Veen
Gerald Parks
Editorial Assistant: P. A. Mantey
Design: Steve Lopez

Photo Credits:
©1997 PhotoDisc, Inc.: Cover, 1, 4, 26, 56, 64, 74, back cover;
©1997 Image Farm, Inc.: Cover, 1, 3, 4, 5, back cover; Cleo Photos: 16, 36;
Gail Denham: 46; D. Jeanene Tiner: 84; Jim Whitmer: 7.

©1997 by the Gospel Publishing House
Springfield, Missouri 65802-1894

International Standard Book Number 0-88243-122-6
Printed in the United States of America

A Leader's Guide for individual or group study with this book is available
(order number 02-0222).

Contents

STUDY   PAGE

1 The Roots Of Codependency 7
2 Understanding Codependency 16
3 Making Your World Right 26
4 The Avoidance Response 36
5 The Healing Process 46
6 The Balancing Act 56
7 The Brain And Codependency 64
8 Myths Of Codependency 74
9 The Final Steps 84

Welcome To The
SPIRITUAL *Discovery* SERIES

We are glad you have chosen to study with us. We believe the discoveries you make through the use of the *Spiritual Discovery Series* will positively impact your life.

The *Spiritual Discovery Series* will challenge the user to ask questions of the biblical text, discover principles from the text, and make personal application of those truths. The Bible is the text. This guide is a tool for study.

The *Spiritual Discovery Series* is designed for use in either individual or group settings. Individuals will be excited by the discoveries made possible through a structured inductive study. Sunday School classes and other groups will find the *Spiritual Discovery Series* a valuable tool for promoting enlightened discussions centered on biblical truth.

How To Use This Study Guide

1 **Pray before beginning each study session.** Ask the Holy Spirit to illuminate your mind.

2 **Choose a translation of the Bible which you trust and can understand.** It will be helpful to have more than one translation available to aid your understanding of the biblical text.

3 **The Bible is your primary text.** Avoid using commentaries or reference books until after completing your own study. Reference works are best used to confirm your findings. On occasion, the study guide will direct you to use reference material. This is done when special insights are necessary for proper interpretation.

4 **Read the assigned biblical text at least twice before answering any questions.** This will provide an overview and focus on God's Word.

5 **Concentrate on the biblical passage which you are studying.** It is tempting to jump from one passage of Scripture to another in an attempt to make spiritual connections.

6 **Seek tangible ways to apply the principles gleaned from each study.** Bible study should never result in "head knowledge" alone. Bible study should lead to action.

BEFORE YOU BEGIN THE SESSION

The subject of codependency is intensely private. If you are using this Study Guide in a group setting, it is important that you are committed to unity and confidentiality within your group. These elements are essential to recovery. A "Confidentiality Agreement" is included with the Leader's Guide and might be given to you to complete. Allow yourself to develop trust in your fellow group members, and share your feelings with them to begin recovery.

STUDY 1

THE ROOTS OF CODEPENDENCY

What is *codependency*? In simple terms it is a pattern of unhealthy involvement in personal relationships. The result is to become *dependent* on the behaviors of those with whom a common relationship is shared.

Codependency is one of the most common forms of dependent behavior, presenting itself in countless variations and patterns. Every codependent's experience is both different and similar.

Codependency can be as simple as a progressive nuisance in our lives, or it may be a devastating and even deadly disorder. As we shall see, Christians are peculiarly vulnerable to it.

During the course of the following studies we will take a thorough look at what causes codependency, and how we can best escape its effects.

THE STRUGGLE FOR RIGHTEOUSNESS

The more his 42-year-old father struggled with chronic alcoholism, the more John fought to save both him and the family business that depended so much on his father's experience. He dreamed of helping his father return to the way he used to be before the serious drinking had started. But all of his efforts were to no avail, and it was clear that the next trip to the hospital for detoxification might be the last.

John tried everything he could think of. He scarcely let his father out of his sight, and if his father did sneak a drink, he hunted until he found the bottle and immediately emptied it. He would often argue with his father about the alcohol abuse and what it was doing to him and his family.

Time was taking its toll. John was beginning to break under the stress of salvaging the business and trying to keep his father sober. Not only was he losing touch with himself, but he felt strangely compelled to ponder what had always been unimaginable to him. Maybe he should drink a little, just to cope.

Like John, those who have just begun to understand the impact codependency has upon their lives may be eager to break free of it. But the road out of codependency is a road of faith, and we must first travel over some unfamiliar ground on the way to freedom.

Our journey to recovery begins in the last place you might ever think to look—personal frailty.

Committed Christians generally have a deep desire to excel in service to their Lord and King. The Bible teaches that Christians should be dedicated to God's service. Yet while pursuing righteousness, it is easy to miss the important counsel Scripture gives us about human shortcomings and to overlook the impact our personal frailty has on our own lives and the lives of those around us.

We cannot make solid progress in our recovery from codependency unless we constantly acknowledge our limitations and our need of God's strength and help. Recovery from codependency requires personal involvement. Just reading about codependency will not necessarily bring change, any more than casually reading the Scripture will bring change.

1. Read Romans 3:23. What does this passage tell us is the basis of the struggle we face to live a righteous life?

_____

_____

_____

Our human frailties affect us in many ways. Even as Christians we fail to do all of what we are supposed to do and oftentimes we do that which we are not supposed to. This is especially true in relationships. We routinely fail to love without reserve, forget to forgive, hesitate to serve, balk at profound sacrifice, and neglect our calling as peacemakers and servants.

The Word of God instructs us to rejoice "in" our sufferings, not "because of" them (Romans 5:3). We are to move beyond a point of self-pity and allow God to work in and through our circumstance(s) to make us better people. Our dependency must be on Him.

✎ 2. Read Romans 7:18,19. In his letter to the Romans, Paul is very straightforward about how he sees his level of personal righteousness. How does he see himself?

Paul's desire to do good ___ Very High ___ High ___Average ___ Low ___ Deficient

Personal righteousness ___ Very High ___ High ___Average ___ Low ___ Deficient

What does Paul see as the basis of his dilemma? _____

_____

✎ 3. Read Ecclesiastes 7:20 and James 2:10. What is the result when people feel they have the ability to live righteously in their own strength?

_____

Rarely will Christians declare they have no sin. Yet many Christians forget their vulnerability to sin because their new life is so different from the old. Being aware of our sin nature is crucial not only to our faith, but to our recovery.

The next few questions are personal. It is important to prayerfully consider each question and respond honestly. If writing your answers makes you uncomfortable, simply think about your response to each of the following questions.

✎ 4. Read Romans 7:14-25.

a. What are the major shortcomings in your life? _____

_____

_____

_____

b. Is there any area in your life where you live your faith to perfection? Explain.

_____

_____

_____

c. How does your answer to question (a) compare to what Paul might have answered?

_____

_____

_____

_____

✎ 5. Review Romans 7:18. It took courage for Paul to acknowledge his frailty in the world of legalism in which he lived. Why did he do it?

_____
_____
_____
_____

Our sin nature never takes a vacation. It forever attempts to secure a foothold in our lives and to draw us away from God. We may fool ourselves into thinking sin is not a problem for us, but that is because we look only at obvious shortcomings. Since God has set a high standard of obedience, sin can occur at a very low threshold. It is not just abstaining from sins of major proportions, it is the failure to share something as small as a moment of compassion. (See Matthew 10:42.)

✎ 6. What reality does Ecclesiastes 7:22 make us face? In Matthew 7:12, what standard does Jesus set for us to be righteous?

_____
_____
_____

It is hard to do everything right! Imagine yourself discussing an incident in which some other church members got caught in a conflict. As you discuss the situation, you gradually point out certain characteristics of one of the people who seemed to have started the problem. You have begun to gossip and to pass judgment! Like many human frailties, the process starts subtly, then engages our hearts before we have a chance to break free.

✎ 7. Read Genesis 4:7. Think of a specific sin you struggle with. Describe where the subtle, progressive pattern of sin began in that situation.

_____
_____
_____
_____

Did you recognize the progression when it started, or did it take you by surprise?

_____
_____

When you first recognized the pattern was it easy or difficult to stop?

What course of action did you take?

Our struggle with human frailties and shortcomings is one we cannot win by our own efforts. The Bible teaches us that our righteousness comes from God and not from ourselves; from His forgiveness and not from our efforts. For this reason, we are unable to become spiritual in our own strength, to find God in our own strength, to be righteous in our own strength, and do any good thing in our own strength alone. (See Philippians 3:9.)

8. Read 2 Corinthians 12:8-10. In what ways was Paul powerless over his situation? How did his circumstances affect his life decisions?

What other alternatives could Paul have taken when faced with his own powerlessness?

How does our powerlessness relate to sinful progressions in our lives? Do we always need God's deliverance, or can we overcome sinful action and attitudes simply because we are Christians, we have confessed our sin, and have the desire to change?

9. Read Isaiah 64:6-9 (NIV). Isaiah states that our sins can sweep us away and that our righteous acts are worthless. We seem out of control. According to verse 7, how do we get to this state?

What hope does Isaiah 64:8,9 provide? _____

THE DILEMMA OF DENIAL

Denial is the failure to acknowledge shortcomings or negative life events and to deal with them in an appropriate and timely manner. All of us have denial in our lives.

Understanding our many frailties is crucial to our faith, for if we fail to see our shortcomings, we are unlikely to address them or overcome them. Without recognizing our tendency toward failure, we will overlook God's forgiveness and mercy and trust in our own efforts, rather than in His righteousness. Without forgiveness, we run the risk of trying to fix our own failures or giving up entirely.

Is there any area in your life for which you have given up asking God for help?

✎ 10. Read Proverbs 20:9. In our culture people prefer to see themselves in positive terms. Compare this philosophy with the biblical view. Does it produce denial? Explain.

_____
_____
_____
_____

The Bible provides many instructions regarding our personal conduct. These instructions come through Old Testament law, the patriarchs, the prophets, kings, and Jesus himself. All of these instructions are summed up in the two great commandments: To love God with all of your heart, mind, soul, and strength, and to love your neighbor as yourself (Mark 12:31). Many times in our Christian walk we fall short of the great calling of our faith. At the same time we often fail to look at these failures. This is denial. All of us practice denial—not necessarily with intention, we just do it. It is impossible to keep track of all our shortcomings.

✎ 11. Read Psalm 19:12,13 and 1 John 1:8-10. What are we instructed to do concerning our shortcomings?

_____
_____

What are some common forms of denial? Overworking, overeating, procrastinating, lack of exercise, lack of prayer, failure to share resources with the world's poor, and lack of ministry to those in need are just a few.

✏️ 12. Read Matthew 22:37-40. Do you have any denial related to the commandments you just read? Which one is the hardest for you? Either record your answer below or make it a personal matter of prayer.

_____

_____

_____

_____

✏️ 13. Explain your response to each part of this item. When you acknowledge denial, does it cause you to:

Be more thankful for God's forgiveness? _____

_____

Think you can overcome any shortcomings? _____

_____

Make you lean on God's mercy more? _____

_____

Make you more judgmental? _____

_____

Make you less judgmental? _____

_____

Many Scriptures address our human frailty. Recognizing our frailty is not to disregard it, nor to excuse it, but rather to understand our perpetual need of the Cross and the righteousness of Jesus. Without understanding our frailty we may presume more of ourselves than we should. We may see ourselves as having great faith rather than little faith. As a consequence we may lean less on the Lord and more on our own human frailty.

What does our spiritual need have to do with codependency? Our recovery from codependency is based on faith. It is not that God will correct another person's shortcomings, but that He will correct our own. One of the surprising lessons of recovery from dysfunctional behavior is not what is wrong with the world around us, or with people who have made our lives difficult, but to understand what those difficulties have caused to be wrong within us. It is not to keep a record of unjust treatment, but to review how others' unfairness to us makes us unfair to others. Sensitivity to our own need for maturation leads us to spiritual growth and recovery from dependency.

✎ **14. Honestly evaluate your present spiritual condition with the following scale:**

I tend to see my faith as Strong ____ Weak ____ Moderate ____

Denial of our own shortcomings is a common occurrence when we are in the process of being mistreated or neglected in our relationships with friends, family, and acquaintances, or if we have received such treatment in the past.

What makes such denial hard to detect is that it is easier to spot shortcomings in another person than to see them in ourselves; to see how another person hurts us rather than how we hurt others.

✎ **15. Without being critical of yourself, answer these questions:**

What dysfunctions or shortcomings do you have that affect other people? _____

_____

_____

_____

When you experience stress, exhaustion, or emotional pain do your own dysfunctions impact other people more than when you're not experiencing those situations? Explain.

_____

_____

_____

_____

SUMMARY

During the course of each of our studies of codependency, we will discuss the mystery of recovery. The term *recovery* means different things to different people, so we will proceed with a basic definition.

Recovery for the Christian occurs when God helps us each day to cope with the effects of unhealthy relationships in a way that honors His will and is dependent upon Him. Recovery is a gift in which we must forever live. It reflects His strength in us.

In this study, we have discovered that we cannot win the battle of codependency alone. As hard as we try, our righteous actions will not set us free from the behavior which ensnares us.

An equally futile means of dealing with codependent activities is denial. We must first admit our sin before we are able to deal appropriately with it and live in a state of recovery.

Let's Review

✏️ 1. What is sin?

_____
_____
_____
_____

✏️ 2. Where does righteousness come from?

_____
_____
_____
_____

✏️ 3. Who has honored the great commandments 100% every day?

_____
_____
_____
_____

✏️ 4. What is denial? What is the appropriate way to deal with it?

_____
_____
_____
_____
_____

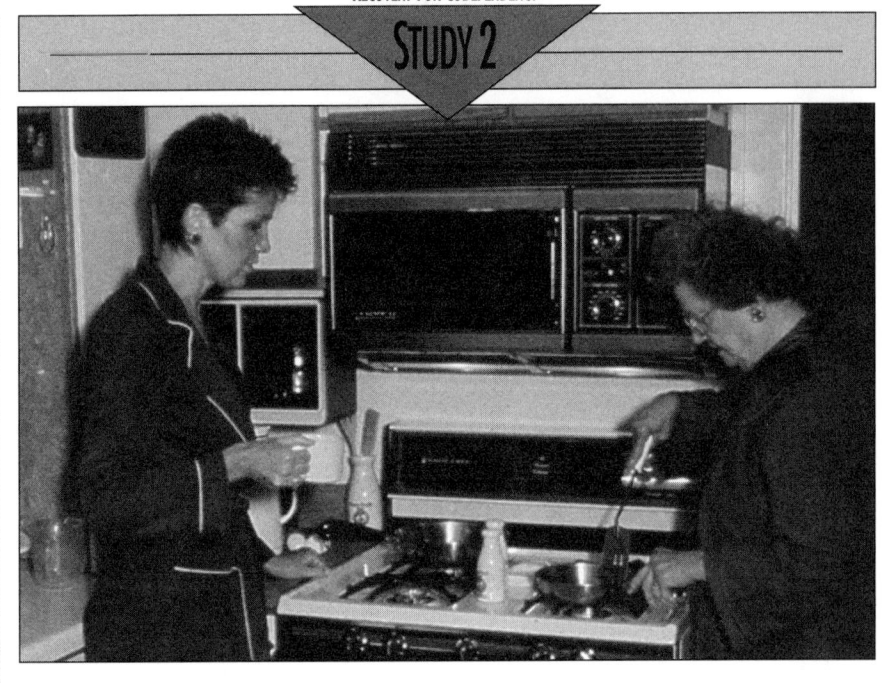

UNDERSTANDING CODEPENDENCY

Now that we have looked at the problem of human frailty, we will begin to address the types of codependency and its progression.

Codependency is just one of many things in our lives that are "unmanageable." Codependency is not the kind of problem we can just overcome by will power alone—we need God's help.

How can we detect codependency? Some basic signs of codependency may include the following:

* To live dependent upon the actions of others.
* To have emotional scarring from involvement in unhealthy relationships with those around us.
* To try to "fix" other people when we really should leave them alone.
* To unintentionally bring harm to others by virtue of our personal shortcomings.
* To have unhealthy personal boundaries.

TYPES OF DEPENDENCY

A frequent result of codependency is that the quality of our Christian life is compromised, and in the process we may unintentionally harm others, even people we love or want to help!

Some dependency is a necessary part of our human existence. No person is an island, and even the most isolated hermit depends on "things" made by others in order to survive.

We must balance our independence with our need for others. We depend on government, social systems, friends, and family. In fact, without people around us with whom we feel somewhat safe, we would be under constant health-destroying stress, unable to rest or recuperate.

✎ 1. Read Matthew 6:25-33 regarding our dependency upon God. Recall a special instance where God met your need.

_____

_____

_____

Assess in what ways you depend on others to fulfill the following needs:

Social needs; i.e., friendship, family support_____

_____

_____

Emotional needs; i.e., purpose, being valued _____

_____

_____

Physical needs; i.e., food, shelter_____

_____

_____

Spiritual needs; i.e., peace, strength _____

_____

_____

In our society, many people see themselves as unique, independent, and overcoming the world around them, even though they are, in reality, dependent on friends and social systems like everyone else. We all have dependencies.

It can be hard to draw a line between dependencies which are healthy and necessary and those dependencies where we lean too much on our support systems and not enough on God. Every Christian's life is different. John the Baptist lived in the wilderness with no luxuries. God provided for him. Yet God also has Christians take care of one another, as in the case of the Early Church widows (Acts 6:1-4).

How much should we depend on others and how much should they depend on us? Only God knows, for dependency is something God needs to direct and control in our lives. Yet we always need to remember that our final dependency is on the Good Shepherd.

Daily Dependencies

In recovery from codependency, it is important to be aware of our dependencies, so we can learn to trust God more in dealing with them.

2. Read Psalm 68:5; John 15:13,14; and 1 Corinthians 1:9. How does God minister to our daily needs?

_____

_____

Social needs: We all have need of some companionship, but since each of us is different we learn to depend on different social support systems.

3. Do you feel more comfortable around:

        A few friends ____ Small groups ____ Large Groups ____

Do you feel more comfortable:

        Alone ____ In groups ____

Emotional needs: Each of us is different emotionally. For instance, some of us need to express our feelings a lot while some of us express relatively little emotion. Some of us need more expressions of support than others do, yet all of us need to feel valued and to have a sense of purpose, and all of us want freedom from depression and other emotional maladies.

4. What emotional circumstances do you require to keep you in your comfort zone?

_____

_____

_____

Physical needs: All of us need protection from physical stress and the environment around us. We need to keep dry and warm in cold weather, and we need shade in hot weather. We need medicines, food, and a comfortable place to rest.

✎ 5. Answer the following questions concerning your physical needs:

What is your greatest physical dependency? _____

What physical dependency do you protect the most? _____

Which physical dependency gives you the most trouble? _____

Spiritual needs: One of the great struggles of the Christian life is to make sure we depend on the Creator rather than simply the people He created. God wants us to depend on Him above everything else, yet He places us in a world where we may also need to depend on those around us.

✎ 6. How do you feel about your relationship with God?

_____

_____

_____

Is there a person you lean on for spiritual support? Identify him or her. _____

_____

Why are you a Christian? _____

_____

_____

Healthy Dependencies

There are many areas in one's life where dependencies play a positive role. Insulin is a healthy dependency for diabetics; without it they would be very ill. Heart medicine is a healthy dependency for heart patients. Friends can be a healthy dependency for someone who is lonely.

Some of our dependencies have worked well for us. We have, for instance, trusted people who have been careful to honor that trust.

✎ 7. List some dependencies you have that are healthy.

_____

_____

_____

What has your experience of dependency on God been like? _____

_____

Do you find yourself depending more or less on Him today? Why? _____

_____

_____

✎ 8. Read each verse below and write what we can depend on God for.

Psalm 73:24 _____

_____

1 Corinthians 10:13 _____

_____

Ephesians 1:2,7 _____

_____

Ephesians 3:17-19 _____

_____

Depending on God may mean to depend on those He has provided to help us, while in the background depending on Him. Depending on God may mean trusting Him to take us through trials and difficulties in our lives through which He wants us to grow.

Unhealthy Dependencies

In the stress of everyday living, it is easy to lean on circumstances or relationships that seem to offer security and comfort. But this is a problem. As we lean on the world's support systems (which God may have given to us), it is very easy to lean too much or too often. We may find ourselves leaning on people and support systems that God never meant for our lives, or leaning in a way that has become unhealthy.

✎ 9. Read Galatians 6:1-5. What balance does Paul suggest regarding assisting people in their struggles?

_____

_____

_____

Another unhealthy attitude can be our defensiveness. This sign of unhealthy dependency is a reluctance to look at a particular area of our lives. When we become locked into an unhealthy dependency, we often don't want to think about a character flaw, much less change!

✎ 10. Can you think of relationships or circumstances where you began to trust the world around you rather than God? List some below.

_____

_____

_____

Ask yourself the following questions.
* Am I aware of emotional dependency I may have on someone I shouldn't?
* Is there someone I depend on too much?
* Does that dependency prevent me from depending on God?
* How do I know when my dependency on someone is healthy?
* How do I know when my dependency on someone is out of God's will?
* Does the idea that I may have an unhealthy dependency make me defensive?

Addictive Dependencies
Before we proceed we need to develop a working definition of dependency as it relates to addiction.

In the addiction field, the term *dependency* is commonly used to identify the way an addict becomes dependent upon a drug or drugs in order to function. In this context, dependency has the same meaning as addiction. Similarly, codependency is also known as coaddiction.

If we are to understand what motivates and affects the codependent or coaddict, we must also look at the dependent or addict to whom they are responding.

Addicts and dependents are not just people who are dependent on street drugs. Addicts can be dependent on adrenaline surges, as in the case of the rageaholic, risktaker, gambler, or even the habitual bungee jumper (all of which are "adrenaline junkies").

They can also be dependent on other life-controlling patterns such as:
* Compulsive spending.
* Eating disorders.
* Manipulative personalities.
* Overcontrol of people (control junkies).
* Workaholism.
* Cult mentalities.
* Living for emotional drama (as typified by modern soap operas).

It is possible to become codependent to any of the "addictions" listed above and many others.

STAGES OF CODEPENDENCY

Stage 1: Denial And Minimizing
To *deny* a problem means we either refuse to look at it, or if we do look at it, decline to do anything about it in a timely, effective way. *Minimization* is a form of denial in which we fail to accept the seriousness of a problem.

Codependency progresses rapidly in the presence of minimization and denial. How does denial work? Think of the codependent husband, wife, son, or daughter who has a family member with a drug problem or a rage problem. He or she loves the family member and desperately wants to help him or her with the problem. The codependent person attempts to do his or her best, but after a few days nothing has really changed. Instead of acknowledging something is very wrong and beyond his or her control, the codependent person creates flimsy explanations as to why he or she failed or why the problem will not occur again. Excuses often include:

"It was a one-time incident."
"He was just having a bad day."
"She promised never to do it again."
"He'll listen to me and stop doing it if I really let him know I'm serious."
"I won't let her get near any more alcohol."

11. Denial/Minimization Inventory. Answer the following questions to the best of your ability. Explain your responses.

Have you ever given up trying to solve a problem that led to a troubled relationship and decided to simply run away from it?

_____

_____

_____

Have you ever convinced yourself that a difficult relationship was not as bad as it really was?

_____

_____

_____

Have you ever felt like you shouldn't express your true feelings in a relationship?

_____

_____

_____

Stage 2: Isolation

Isolation occurs when we avoid people or situations where the unwanted behaviors of a dysfunctional relationship might "erupt." For example, Bill never takes his family out to social functions where alcohol can be accessed, because he is afraid of what his alcoholic wife will do. The family is stuck at home with the problem.

Unfortunately, when we try to control an addict's behavior, we often shield him or her from the consequences of that behavior, which in turn supports his or her drinking and protects the addiction.

✏️ **12. How have you isolated yourself, your family, or your friends to prevent that person's addictive behavior from being disruptive to you?**

_____

_____

_____

How has protecting the addict's behavior forced you to change your lifestyle?

_____

_____

_____

How have changes in your lifestyle affected relationships with family and friends?

_____

_____

_____

Stage 3: Breakdown

After an extended period of trying to cope with an addict, we may finally come to the conclusion that the situation is hopeless. By this time our relationship with the addict has caused us some damaging stress. Our behaviors start to change. We are always on guard, trying to protect ourselves from unpredictable behavior. We may try to escape the relationship only to discover that we cannot.

✏️ **13. How do you feel when nothing seems to work in your relationship with an addict and his or her behavior?**

_____

_____

What support systems do you have in place to help you cope with your life situation?

_____

_____

_____

Stage 4: Escape

After a certain point in time, everyone's instinct is to escape. *I have to get away at all costs*, we think. We may move to another town, change jobs, or just stay extremely busy. Sometimes escape is the only practical solution, yet escape carries with it three possible dangers:

* Danger One

We may escape from a situation that God wanted us to grow through.

* Danger Two

We may escape from a situation, only to discover the unhealthy dependent relationships we developed continue to shape our lives and relationships with people in the place to which we escaped. We can easily fall into another codependent relationship and experience the cycle of destruction all over again.

* Danger Three

We may fail to deal with our emotional wounds.

Escape is rarely the ideal resolution we expect.

14. **Have you ever escaped from what you felt was an unhealthy situation? Explain.**

_____

_____

What might God have done if you had stayed?

_____

_____

What scars do you carry from staying in an unhealthy situation?

_____

_____

_____

SUMMARY

The progression of codependency in our lives easily develops into an addiction. Understanding the motivating factors behind dependent behavior will help us to break the habit of a codependent relationship or circumstance. We must not deny nor detract from the seriousness of our problem(s). Facing our issues is of paramount concern in the recovery process, and must be in direct combination with the healing power of the Lord Jesus Christ. It is by His power alone that we can overcome a codependent relationship or behavior.

LET'S REVIEW

✎ 1. What are some basic signs of codependency?

✎ 2. List some examples of healthy dependencies.

✎ 3. What makes a dependency unhealthy?

✎ 4. What are the four stages of codependency?

✎ 5. What dangers are involved in escaping an addictive situation?

MAKING YOUR WORLD RIGHT

Despite our best intentions, it is very easy to be caught up in unhealthy relationships. Few of us live in a world where everyone around us is sweet and wonderful, and certainly not everyone we meet is concerned about our personal well-being.

Some of us grow up surrounded by trouble. There are areas in our society where disproportionate numbers of homes are broken and dysfunctional. Some of the children from those homes grow up to be members of churches.

Even the people that love us have personal problems which sometimes end up on our "doorstep." We may become codependent to any of these loved ones as well as those who don't love us at all!

FIXING OR FACILITATING

Who are the people to whom we become codependent? Some are obvious to us: the manager or boss who brings their emotional problems to work and then dumps them on the employees; the alcoholic mother who neglects and frightens her children; the father who rages and abuses his children, turning his home into an emotional "armed camp."

Some are not so obvious. The friend whose manipulative behavior always gets you to do something you didn't want to do. Later you feel used and wonder why you didn't say something. The coworker who subtly intimidates you. The church lay leader who makes you feel guilty whenever you don't work at the church.

We cannot avoid every difficult relationship in our lives. We cannot change families, churches, and jobs every time a relationship with someone causes us stress. On the other hand, if we stay in stressful relationships, they will always have some effect on us. Some of those effects can be serious, especially over time.

Positive codependency usually begins when the codependent tries to "fix" or adjust whatever he or she perceives to be wrong with another person. This is the "buying in" stage. Whether we intend to or not, once the fixing process starts, we become emotionally involved. At this point, a codependent relationship has begun. This emotional involvement can simply cause us stress, or it can eventually get us into emotional difficulties ourselves, fostering more unhealthy relationships and preventing us from being the healthy Christian God wants us to be.

We may be highly motivated to help other people, but when we become engaged in a dysfunctional relationship with nothing more than a positive attitude, or the determination to "fix" that other person, the initial result is more often entrapment than progress. The harder we work at the relationship, the more resistance there is, and the harder it becomes to change or fix the other person. This pattern is positive codependency. It is codependency in its most common form.

Once we begin to fix and attempt to control one person, it is very easy to try to fix others. Soon we may be trying to control many relationships in the way we think is best, rather than the way God wants.

Remember: codependent relationships commonly start when we are caught in a relationship with an addicted person.

Vulnerability

The Christian has some special challenges in facing difficult relationships. We have to tolerate, forgive, and even love in return for mistreatment. Loving, caring, and taking healthy responsibility are often confused with codependent responses. It can be hard to know when supporting someone is helping them or hurting them!

1. Read Matthew 5:39-42. Based on the following scenarios, imagine yourself in the same situation, and apply the standards Jesus gives us for response to mistreatment. (Hint: Be realistic rather than idealistic.)

A. A worker in a factory who daily faces a verbally abusive and tyrannical supervisor.

_____

B. A housewife who faces the chaos of an alcoholic husband.

_____

C. A church deacon trying to help someone who repeatedly uses and manipulates him/her.

D. An adult experiencing the childhood scars of neglect.

We are to respond to others as Jesus has instructed us in Matthew 5:39-42, yet we have to be careful not to fall into a codependent situation.

2. Read Matthew 5:41. This Scripture teaches we should go the "extra mile." What does this concept mean to you practically in regard to helping another person?

Here are three typical responses to the command to go an extra mile:
* Cautious - "I don't want to make the problem worse."
* Passive - "Maybe this problem will blow over."
* Aggressive - "Maybe I can help the person correct the problem."

3. Does one of the above responses come close to your experience? Which one and why?

4. Read John 16:33. What does Jesus warn us about in this passage? What promise does He provide?

We will engage many unhealthy and difficult relationships ranging from an encounter with a playground bully to facing a mentally troubled family member.

Many people make the erroneous assumption that codependent relationships can be fixed. But not every problem in life can be resolved, and not every difficult situation can be escaped. God does not promise to remove our difficulties, in fact, He promises to allow us difficulties as a means of growth. One of the most difficult problems we face in codependent relationships is to determine exactly what God wants for us in a particular situation. If we ran from every bad relationship in the fear we might become codependent, we could never function. If we stayed in every situation, no matter how bad, we could be destroyed. For instance, if a family member is constantly drunk and physically abusive, it is best to get out and seek help.

✏️ 5. Read Romans 12:14-21. What motive should direct our interaction with others?

_____

How could this motive inadvertently misguide us in our relationship with an addict?

_____

_____

How can we assure ourselves that we are doing the right thing?

_____

Christians in very difficult or dangerous relationships eventually realize unless God does a miracle, there is no simple escape short of moving, divorcing, or changing careers. As a result, they may feel the best response is to tolerate mistreatment from the addict. But what is God's will in the situation? Only He knows what is the best solution.

A good exercise for determining correct action is to carefully think through what will probably happen rather than giving way to imagined fears. What might actually happen (not just your worst fears) if you left the bad relationship now? Would God still take care of you?

✏️ 6. Read Psalm 138:7 and Jeremiah 10:23,24. What hope do these verses give to those who step out in faith not knowing fully if they are right or wrong?

_____

✏️ 7. Read Psalms 37:5; 119:105; Proverbs 1:5. How do we know when it is unhealthy and not in God's will to stay in a stressful situation? How does God lead you personally?

_____

_____

_____

The Tendency To Fix

As we have mentioned, the most common dilemma we face with positive codependency is the instinct to "fix" the other person. "Fixing" should be differentiated from ministry and correction. "Fixing" implies the effort to manipulate or pressure another person to change. Ministry to a person and godly correction reflect a humble effort to support change in God's time and way.

To see how limited the "fixing" response is, look back at your own life. Can it be easily "fixed"? Can you be everything you want to be? Do you immediately correct every failure in your life?

When another person has a glaring fault (at least glaring to us), it seems they should be able to change, especially with our support. Yet they cannot always change. They cannot always see their faults. It is God who changes and fixes, not us.

✎ 8. Read Matthew 7:3-5. What instruction does Jesus give in regard to "fixing" others?

_____

_____

✎ 9. Read Romans 14:4. What does this Scripture tell us about God's investment in the success of others?

_____

✎ 10. Read Psalm 51:10 and Ephesians 1:18. Who is able to change a person's heart?

_____

✎ 11. Read John 3:17. Ask yourself the following questions when you try too hard to "fix" or "save" another person:

Who loves this person the most, God or me? _____

Who is working the hardest to help him or her, God or me? _____

All of us have a tendency to attempt to fix other people. Even if we are not able to correct a situation, we wish we could!

✎ 12. Complete the following statement. "It bothers me when someone else..."

_____

_____

Examples of things that bother people include being insensitive, talking too much, living unhealthily, being untruthful, driving recklessly, or saying inappropriate things.

✎ 13. What is the reason these things bother you? What are you trying to do when you complain and try to change these behaviors in others?

_____

_____

HELPING OR HURTING

A subtle problem surfaces when we attempt to fix people instead of allowing God to do it. We begin a task we can never finish. It would seem if we try to help someone and fail, it would still be worth trying. But there is a hidden problem with this strategy. If we try to help someone who is not ready to change, they may resist the help, and then it will be even harder to reach them. Our efforts may simply cause them to entrench their behavior. In this way our efforts can quickly make the problem worse.

Enabling

Over and over the codependent thinks, "If I can just change this circumstance, or demonstrate this point, the addict will change his or her ways."

Sometimes we have a false sense of control over the addict that comes from a false sense of control over our own lives. Many times during the process of recovery, we need to return to the fact we are powerless.

14. Read James 4:13-15. What do we have power over?

_____

Enabling is any means, intentional or not, by which we increase the addict's problem by trying to help. A typical scenario is the housewife who hides liquor bottles from her alcoholic husband to keep him from drinking too much. The result is that he simply works harder to protect his supply of alcohol from his wife. His drinking becomes worse.

15. Review your relationship with an addict or a dependent person. Have you tried to change his or her behavior? If yes, what effort did it take and what was the long-term result?

_____

_____

_____

_____

Rescuing And Caretaking

Martha's husband is an alcoholic. It is Monday morning and her husband Marty is too sick from the weekend's drinking to get out of bed. So she calls his boss to say that Marty has the flu and won't be able to come in.

What Martha is doing is called rescuing or caretaking. By protecting her husband from the consequences of his drinking, she is making it safe for him to continue drinking.

Martha reasons if her husband loses his job, it will hurt her as much as him. But if Marty is an alcoholic, he might eventually lose his job anyway, or get sued in a traffic accident, or die prematurely. On the other hand, if Marty loses his job, he may be forced to get help for his drinking.

How is Martha to know what to do? How do we know when and when not to rescue?

✎ **16. Read Proverbs 3:6. What does it mean to acknowledge God?**

_____

_____

How have you "rescued" people? _____

_____

_____

Adjusting
One of the most common responses to living with or around an addict is to try to adjust to the problem. Whatever the addict does, the codependent adjusts to it. For instance, if the addict rages, the coaddict simply tries to remain calm and keep the situation calm. Unfortunately, the person who adjusts to the addict makes it easier for the addict to run out of control. This is another form of enabling.

What form of adjusting do you use the most?

Being The Hero
Many times the codependent avoids some of the pitfalls we have mentioned, only to become the family hero. In this role, the codependent works hard at excellence in lifestyle, to help overshadow the bad influence of the addict. The warmth and effort of this codependent draws attention away from the addict.

Yet in trying to help the family this way, the codependent often loses touch with reality and encounters his or her own set of emotional problems.

✎ **17. Read Psalm 127:1. What is the result of our best efforts?**

_____

How have you tried to be the hero? _____

_____

_____

RELIEF OR WRECKAGE

Frustration
When every effort we make fails to change another person, we may find ourselves increasingly angry at the addict. We may want them to change whether it is God's time for them to change or not. If we think we can control another person, our anger is sure to increase if our efforts to control fail.

✎ 18. Read Ephesians 4:26. Anger is part of life, but what does the Scripture suggest we do with it?

___

Stress

Dealing with the uncertainties, mood swings, broken promises, and mistreatment by addicted people takes a toll on us, but that toll is multiplied when we are co-addicted (trying to control the addict's behavior).

✎ 19. What signs of emotional stress do you have? (Examples may include: depression, anxiety, burnout, mood swings, fearfulness, anger.)

___

___

___

✎ 20. What signs of physical stress do you have? (Examples may include: headaches, anxiety, stomach upset/tension, nervous twitches, exhaustion, or intestinal discomfort.)

___

___

___

Progression

Have you ever tried to fix something with the wrong tool or accomplish too big a task with the wrong equipment? As a result, you worked far harder than if you had taken time to go and get the right tool or equipment. It is the same with unhealthy responses in our lives. We end up working harder and harder to accomplish only a little task. This pattern is especially true of codependency. The more we push the addict, the less progress we tend to make, but the more commitment we make to solving the problem. We simply get deeper into our control patterns. Our codependency progresses.

✎ 21. Read Matthew 8:5-10. When you try harder to control, is that greater faith or less faith? Explain.

___

___

___

___

How is your control behavior stronger than when you began? Are you trying harder now, but seeing little result? Why do you think this is the case?

_____
_____
_____
_____

Living As Victims

There is always the danger as our codependency takes hold that we will fall prey to self-pity. We may persuade ourselves that life is treating us unfairly. Forgetting who is in charge of our life, or who is supposed to be, we become victims.

✎ 22. Read John 5:1-8 and think about Jesus' question in verse 6. Here are some hard questions to ask yourself:

How fully do you believe that God is shepherding your life? _____
_____

Are you willing to trust God without trying to fix your world? Explain. _____
_____
_____
_____

Are you willing to thank God for the addict in your life? Explain. _____
_____
_____
_____

SUMMARY

Philippians 2:13 (NIV): "For it is God who works in you to will and to act according to his good purpose."

Our attempt to fix our world often simply serves to facilitate the addict in our lives. Our attempt to protect ourselves and the addict more often hurts his or her chance of recovery. And our attempt to relieve our own pressure many times leads to a life of stress.

After all is said and done, if we are truly powerless, it is God who must help us solve our problems. We must constantly turn to Him for help rather than to continue trying simply to change our circumstances or the behavior of another person.

Let's Review

1. What are the "warning signs" that we are opening ourselves up to a dependent relationship?

2. What should be the Christian's response when faced with difficult relationships?

3. Matthew 5:41 teaches us to extend ourselves to help others. Has this instruction improved your relationships? How?

4. What does John 3:17 instruct us to do concerning "fixing" someone?

5. What is the best formula for avoiding a codependent relationship? Explain.

STUDY 4

THE AVOIDANCE RESPONSE

One of the saddest results of codependency occurs when a Christian withdraws from doing ministry because of bad experiences with failed relationships. The tendency to give up trying to help or relate to certain kinds of people is *negative codependency*.

It is not uncommon for Christians to make sacrificial efforts to help a struggling friend or acquaintance who is experiencing great emotional difficulty. They may make a great investment of prayer, emotional support, time, and effort trying to help addicts or alcoholics or even someone suffering anxiety, loneliness, financial problems, or depression. When the efforts to help don't work, it can be an unnerving experience.

Negative Experiences

Sometimes the effort to help makes an immediate and obvious difference. Sometimes it does not. Good people can invest heart and soul to help a person, only to find their efforts rejected, wasted or disregarded, even belittled.

Whenever we make a costly investment in someone, only to find the effort disregarded, it is at the least discouraging. Then if the person we are trying to help seems to end up worse off than ever, it can have a very chilling effect on our desire to help the next person. After a few bad experiences, we may find ourselves reluctant to get "burned." We then hesitate to help those in need, even though we know we should!

Negative codependency is to respond to this dilemma by avoiding helping certain kinds of people, and trying to help only those with whom we feel safe and in control. This retreat from ministry or attempting to control painful relationships by avoidance can be a progressing lifestyle problem.

Remember: Just as with positive codependency, negative codependent relationships typically start when we are caught in a difficult relationship with an addicted person.

It would be wonderful if we could reach out to people in need and in turn have them respond to us with warmth and appreciation! But ministry is not so simple. In order for people with dysfunctional behavior to receive "help" from us, they may first have to:

* Consider and accept their own inadequacy.
* Accept our genuineness and humbleness in addressing their problem.
* Decide whether of all the people who give them advice, ours is best.
* Decide whether we are critical or caring.
* Decide whether or not we really understand them.
* Decide whether or not we belong in their "space."

1. What goes through your mind when someone offers you advice you asked for?

_____

_____

_____

What goes through your mind when someone offers you advice you did not ask for?

_____

_____

_____

Some people may respond to efforts to help or change them by playing along, putting on an "appreciation face" until the helping person goes away. But the more the "appreciation face" goes on, the more the codependent tries to help, and the more hidden resistance there will be. Early on, resistance may only be evasive, but in the end it may turn belligerent.

✎ 2. Think back to a time when some well-meaning person tried to help you, but you really wanted to be left alone. Which emotion do you remember best?

        Anger _____ Fear _____ Happiness _____

How did you protect your "space"? _____

_____

_____

_____

Although a person may need help, he or she does not always want to receive help. Thus efforts to help may be unappreciated. Consider this: is it harder to give unwanted help or receive it?

✎ 3. Is it harder to give or receive unwanted help? Explain.

_____

_____

_____

REALISTIC CHRISTIAN SERVICE

✎ 4. In John 20:21 Jesus gives the call for Christian service. How do you think a person accomplishes this task in practical ways?

_____

_____

_____

All of us have different expectations of what it is like to do Christian service. Serving God can be a wonderful and seemingly effortless experience or it can be overwhelmingly difficult. We may have romantic ideas about Christian service or we may be quite realistic.

✎ 5. Do you feel ministry or Christian service is:

    An uncomfortable obligation _____   A joy _____

    A comfortable obligation _____   Other _____

Explain. _____

_____

_____

_____

The goal of coping with negative codependency is not escape from difficult relationships; it is to deal with them in an appropriate way. This may involve adversity.

✎ 6. Read John 16:33. What does this passage tell us about our life here in this world?

_____

_____

_____

With the cross only a short time away, and knowing His disciples would face both hardship and adversity, Jesus gave some crucial instruction to His disciples. While they would have trials and adversity, they would also receive His peace.

As Christians we will certainly experience adversity in doing ministry. We may even find ourselves avoiding certain kinds of ministry, not because God wants us to, but because we feel we should be responded to or treated differently. Being caught in a relationship that leads to codependency, and intentionally entering a relationship that is difficult because God wants us to, are two very different things.

It is important to be realistic about how we perceive Christian service. We need to realize doing ministry can mean embracing difficulty. That difficulty can vary, since everyone has different gifts, and different experiences doing the same kind of work.

✎ 7. In which area of ministry do you feel the greatest comfort? The least comfort?

Greatest	Least
_____ Witnessing	_____ Witnessing
_____ Visiting the sick	_____ Visiting the sick
_____ Visiting the imprisoned	_____ Visiting the imprisoned
_____ Teaching	_____ Teaching
_____ Counseling	_____ Counseling

Of course, how we feel about ministry does not necessarily reflect our faith. The Christians in the Roman Coliseum may have been uncomfortable in their role as witnesses, but they certainly had faith. What is most important in coping with codependency is that we understand our feelings as we do ministry, so they do not compromise our effectiveness.

✎ 8. Answer this tough question candidly: "What do I fear most in doing ministry?"

_____
_____
_____

✎ 9. Remember a time when you were trying to do Christian service, ministry, or outreach, and your experience was negative. Briefly describe the emotion you experienced.

_____
_____
_____
_____

We will have adversity in this life, yet we should not let it keep us from any ministry God has for us to do.

MINISTRY: WHEN TO SAY YES—WHEN TO SAY NO

Despite the negative experiences we may have had in ministry, we can never quit. We must "keep on keeping on." So while we are healing from difficult experiences with others, we need to continue in difficult relationships where God may lead us.

✎ 10. Read Matthew 5:39. What instructions does Jesus offer as we minister to others?

_____
_____
_____

In this Scripture, Jesus gives instructions that will clearly lead to our being taken advantage of. Of course, we do not like being taken advantage of. In fact, when we discover someone has taken advantage of us or wounded us, we may be very reluctant to allow ourselves to be hurt again. We may be convinced there is no one we can completely trust. The only way out of this dilemma is to closely follow the Good Shepherd. We must trust God to lead us into and out of relationships at His choosing. We periodically need to examine our lives to discover whether we are doing simply what we want or what God truly wants.

It is true if we are following after Jesus, and He puts in our path someone who will take advantage of us for His purpose, there is not much we can do to protect ourselves but to run from Jesus—and that is no protection! In Job 2:10 (NIV), we encounter Job's stunning observation when he considers the difficulties God has brought him to, "Shall we accept good from God and not trouble?"

We must be certain when we say no to doing ministry, we are not saying no to serving God.

11. Read Matthew 10:11-16. Explain Jesus' instructions when our efforts to reach out to others are spurned.

___

There are times when God simply has not chosen to continue working with particular people. He does not call us to invest more in relationships. Again, the problem in backing off from doing ministry to particular people must be one that follows the counsel and leading of God.

12. Read Psalm 37:5-7. What formula for dealing with people does this passage describe?

___

13. Think back to a situation where you discontinued trying to help someone who disregarded your efforts to help. As you remember that situation, did you feel:

____ Anger   ____ Resentment   ____ Fear   ____ Discouragement

If God had clearly told you to minister to that person no matter how they responded, how might that have affected your feelings?

___

THE AVOIDANCE RESPONSE

Do you remember a time when you said no to helping someone, but felt right about it? What were your reasons?

_____
_____
_____

We have briefly discussed some problems related to doing ministry in the face of adversity. But despite our best motivation and intention, difficult experiences in doing ministry to, or living with, an addictive person can take a toll on us. Ministry can be stressful and even overwhelming. We need to trust God when the road becomes too difficult!

✎ **14. How do you deal with stress, anxiety, and fear that comes when you try to serve God? Does such stress increase your faith? Explain.**

_____
_____
_____
_____

One way people cope with stress and difficulty in ministry is to isolate and avoid any ministry that is uncomfortable to them. There is often a great gulf between what we would like to do for God and what we are able to do.

Everyone has trouble in some area of ministry. For instance, the person who can relate to anyone on the street may have difficulty in administration, while the administrator may be ineffective in evangelism!

✎ **15. In what areas would you like to reach out more?**

_____
_____
_____

What fears do you have about these areas? _____

_____
_____
_____

Turning It Over To God

✎ 16. Read Psalm 71:14-21. What does the Psalmist tell us concerning our difficulties?

_____

_____

_____

Our human nature struggles with the idea of trust. Consider this tough question.

✎ 17. What do you do to avoid such negative experiences?

_____

_____

_____

One of the strongest instincts we humans have is to control relationships. Why is this instinct important? As we control our lives, we try to control them in ways which will bring the least stress and pain. When we are in difficult relationships, we do the same thing—we try to control them first and then maybe ask God what He wants us to do. It can be very hard to "let go and let God" bring painful relationships into our lives. We need to trust God and let Him control our lives.

To Leave Or To Stay

One of the reasons people avoid dysfunctional relationships is they tend to see themselves as victims needing relief. The best way to get short-term relief is to escape the relationship. Of course, many relationships are abusive or dangerous, and the only appropriate response is to get out quickly and stay out. But many relationships are not so much dangerous as they are dysfunctional, and simply running away from them may not be best for anyone involved. The last thing the avoider (the person leaving a relationship) may consider is the damage such avoidance causes to the person he or she is avoiding and also to himself or herself.

How does the avoider in a relationship hurt the person he or she avoiding? The avoider of an unhealthy relationship has usually begun a pattern of controlling, appeasing, or even subtly retaliating. Whatever the avoider's response is, it becomes an excuse to the other person to continue his or her behavior. Thus the avoider is inadvertently helping to perpetuate the unhealthy relationship. Whenever we respond in a difficult relationship in a way which God does not prefer, we carry some degree of responsibility. While we should not simply blame ourselves for the dysfunctional relationship, neither should we use someone else's character flaws to hide our own.

How does the avoider hurt himself or herself? After a bad experience, the avoider may feel disinclined to become involved with other relationships or persons similar to the one he or she just left. But when we run from relationships in which we are supposed to minister, we fail to grow and the people we are supposed to help do not get our help. Instead they may continue in their dysfunctional behavior, free to progress in it because we won't become involved. What is worse, because we have not dealt in a healthy way with a bad relationship, we are far more likely to walk into another one!

18. What relationships have you run from?

___

What might you do differently if you were in the same situation now?

___

SUMMARY

When we reach out to help other people, we may encounter a negative, or even a violent response. Our immediate and continuing response to that situation will have an extraordinary—possibly eternal—effect on us and the other person. We have a choice to make each and every time we are faced with a similar experience. We can choose to allow God to work in and through us to His glory, or we can turn away from the situation in our own strength and avoid the blessing God would have for us. Let us choose to seek His will for us in every situation and bring Him honor and glory!

LET'S REVIEW

✎ 1. Based on the third step of the "Twelve Steps," what is meant by *God as we understood Him*?

✎ 2. Read Mark 8:34. What does "deny himself" mean to you and your relationships?

✎ 3. According to John 16:33, what are we to expect in our journey on this earth?

✎ 4. How are we to survive as we reach out to a lost and dying generation? (Romans 12:2).

STUDY 5

THE HEALING PROCESS

Codependency is one of many progressive behaviors that may occur in our lives. The idea of progression suggests the more we try to change a behavior in another person, the worse it may get and the more failure will affect us. The more we try to fix or cope with another person's problems, the more likely we are to get entangled. Consider the codependent wife who is married to an alcoholic husband whose drinking is getting progressively worse. She tries valiantly to stop her husband's drinking, increasing her efforts but with decreasing results. The damage to the wife is progressive, taking an ever-increasing emotional and physical toll.

Fear And Anxiety

Codependency can begin at an early age. Children who grow up in dysfunctional homes often continue to carry with them the coping mechanisms they used as youngsters to deal with family problems. The passing of years and emotional maturation do not magically erase these coping mechanisms, which survive as intact codependent behaviors in adulthood.

Codependency can begin during adulthood as well. Adults under stress can learn coping mechanisms that cause them trouble throughout their lives. For instance, an adult who has become codependent to a dysfunctional friend may learn stress coping mechanisms and behaviors which may persist long after the initial codependent relationship is over.

What coping mechanisms does codependency leave behind? To name a few—distrust of feelings, denial of feelings, fear of trusting people, isolation, compulsive behavior, control behavior, or even more codependency.

NOTE: In the following section, we will review a few of the typical experiences felt by those who have been in long-term unhealthy relationships. Some may speak to your memories and experience; others may not. If something does not fit your experience exactly, you may still draw something from it in order to understand the experience of others who may be struggling with that emotion.

1. Read Psalm 34:4. What encouragement does the Psalmist offer to us?

_____

_____

At first glance, one might conclude the path of faith is one unmarked by fear. Yet the reason God addresses our fears is precisely because we have them. Some of these fears we see and others we don't. Some fears from the past surface in moments of vulnerability, some fears are constant, and some fears surface only under back-breaking stress.

God is aware of our limitations: "As a father has compassion on his children, so the Lord has compassion on those who fear him; for he knows how we are formed, he remembers that we are dust" (Psalm 103:13,14, NIV).

Dust is the problem. Many of our fears and anxieties occur in spite of ourselves. For instance, some of the survival areas of the brain are structured to direct fear response when we are under excessive stress. The survival part of our brain motivates fear in us even when we intellectually have no desire to fear. To make matters worse, our survival brain stores some traumatic experiences for life, just waiting for some memory to breathe life back into them. Fear is therefore not just a lack of faith, but a human frailty.

What fear might you expect to occur when you are vulnerable or under stress?

2. Read Hebrews 13:5. What type of fear is responded to here? How has this affected you?

_____

_____

Abandonment Fears

Although God will never leave us, people sometimes do. Children who grow up in addictive families have often had the experience of being left alone, manipulated, emotionally mistreated, and often emotionally abandoned. Growing up in an alcoholic home, Billy rarely saw his father. When his father did come home, it was usually for just 2 or 3 days at a time. His father always made promises, such as, "Tomorrow I will take you to a ball game." But when tomorrow came, Billy's father was too drunk to do anything, even to remember the promise.

All the difficult experiences in addictive homes leave emotional scars. As children from these homes grow older, they may not think of abandonment as an issue, yet it may show up in their lives as fear of loneliness, fear of rejection, or even fear of social vulnerability.

3. List experiences you can remember that may have caused you abandonment fears.

_____

_____

_____

_____

Controlling Behaviors

We are to have self-control (with God's strength) to keep our bodies and minds from yielding to sin. However, we are not to control other people.

4. Read Proverbs 29:11 and 1 Thessalonians 4:3,4. What specific instruction is given in these passages?

_____

_____

_____

_____

It is very common for people to respond to emotionally traumatic events and circumstances by trying to protect themselves from further experiences. Controlling others is one way they may try to protect themselves.

Susan grew up in an abusive and addictive home. When she became an adult, she had a drive deep within her to never allow herself in a situation of vulnerability again. Her friends found it difficult to be around her because she always made sure nothing was said or done in a way she didn't like. She subtly dominated every conversation.

How do we protect ourselves? We may:
* "Manage" relationships to make sure they don't get out of our control.
* Avoid relationships we feel we cannot control.
* Keep our distance from other people, avoiding close relationships.

✏️ 5. List areas you tend to control in relationships.

_____
_____
_____

Do you remember instances when others tried to control you? In what way did they do this and how did it feel?

_____
_____
_____

Intimacy Dysfunction/Boundary Failure

The term *intimacy* has to do with the ability to have a healthy, close relationship with another person. For instance, healthy intimacy allows one person to be the close friend of another without undue expectations, presumptions, or control in that relationship.

Similarly, boundaries have to do with a person's appropriate emotional distance from another person. To neither suffocate nor spurn requires delicate socialization skills learned during the years of maturation.

Addictive families often have problems with boundaries. Children from these homes may lack the internal cues necessary to keep them from becoming entangled with either addicts or non-addict individuals.

One of the disastrous results that occurs with people who grow up in any dysfunctional relationship is the loss of boundary distinctions, making it difficult to have a healthy, close relationship with others. How does this happen?

If, for instance, you grew up in a home where some of the family members were hiding the addictive behavior of another family member, you may have encountered an unwritten code—each family member must "keep quiet" about the concealed behavior. The goal is to protect the family from the embarrassment that would follow the discovery of the addiction by friends, relatives, or even authorities. The result is family members become locked into each other's expectations to maintain the silence and to control the addict. Not only are family members locked into each other, they are also locked into controlling the addict's behavior, or at least compensating for it.

Although family members may be socially close to the addict, they may not be emotionally close in any healthy way. Some days the addicted person may smother family members with affection and other days try to hurt or humiliate them. Children in these types of homes grow up not knowing what is real in relationships: not knowing when to trust, not knowing when to be close, not knowing when to keep emotional distance.

These kids become the kind of adults who get caught up in relationships where they are not appreciated, trying to get too close in a relationship where that closeness is not mutually desired, and often ending up being rejected. In order to heal this deep hurt, the adult with boundary problems may begin the cycle all over again by struggling to become close with another person.

How are personal boundaries broken? Boundaries are violated by suffocating closeness, verbal domination, and unrealistic expectations, or excessive distance and failed responsiveness. Not only does the person with boundary problems struggle to find a healthy way to touch other people's boundaries, but their own personal boundaries are often trampled on by others who may have boundary problems of their own or seek to take advantage of that person.

No matter what our experiences have been growing up, none of us keeps boundaries perfectly.

NOTE: It is very difficult for any of us to see our own frailty. This is especially true with boundary problems; we can rarely see when we expect too much of a relationship or when we manipulate it in some way. This next question, therefore, may need to be answered prayerfully.

6. Have you ever inappropriately crossed another person's boundaries? How did you know when it occurred?

_____

_____

What were the results? _____

_____

_____

7. Are there times someone has crossed your boundaries and you have trusted too much, been too vulnerable, and been hurt or taken advantage of? Explain.

_____

_____

_____

In what ways do you find yourself getting too close to people or closer than the relationship calls for?

_____

_____

_____

In what ways do you find yourself keeping others at too great a distance?

_____

_____

_____

✎ 8. Read Proverbs 3:5,6. In whom are we to trust in our understanding of life?

_____

Solomon makes the powerful statement that we should not depend on our own understanding of life. This principle is particularly true regarding our understanding of personal relationships. We do tend to trust people even though there is no way we can know they are completely trustworthy. All of us fail other people at times, and all of us will be failed by others. There is no individual you can trust completely, but at the same time, we have to trust people every day just to function in society.

Since people aren't completely trustworthy, yet since we do have to trust, how do we protect ourselves?

The answer lies in trusting God. Not only do we need to follow His counsel in our relationships, but our trust in Him needs to run deep. In our hearts we must recognize He will bring us through both difficult and easy relationships: some in which we reap wonderful benefits and others in which we are disregarded or taken advantage of. If we remember the Good Shepherd is always with us, we will trust Him to bring us through relationships, instead of trying to control them for our own protection. We must trust the Shepherd.

✎ 9. How do you feel when you trust God, but He brings you into a difficult relationship?

_____

_____

_____

How do you attempt to deal with those feelings?_____

_____

_____

Boundary problems are hard to detect and very difficult to correct. It is almost impossible to see our own limits. Can anything be done to help us overcome boundaries?

There is hope. Since as children we learn boundaries from imitation, one of the very best ways to learn how to overcome them is to model after someone who has good boundaries. By watching others with good boundaries and relating with them, we can make real progress.

✎ 10. Whom would you choose to model after for healthy boundaries? Why did you choose this person?

_____

_____

Of course, our ultimate example is Jesus. As you read the Bible, you can learn from the caring and healthy way Jesus related to people.

Recognition Of Feelings

Because codependency leaves us with emotional scars that cloud our self-perception, it is very important we learn to understand ourselves. It is too easy to live life telling ourselves how we want to feel, rather than facing how we actually feel.

One good way to understand our feelings is to use the "shoehorn" technique. A shoehorn is a tool you use to get something too big into something too small.

This is how it works. Simply stop all distracting activities for a moment. Stop and experience how you feel, with no explanations or interpretations. Don't evaluate or explain to yourself how you feel, simply feel with no explanations or interpretations. Feel what you feel when you really stop. Now, identify that feeling in one of the following simple terms before you alter it in any way. Use just the one-word feeling of *SCARED*, *ANGRY*, *GOOD*, or *BAD*. Repeat that one-word basic feeling back to yourself.

Why is the process called "shoehorning"? Our instinct is to feel our feelings in a way that may be more preferable to us, rather than accurate. Thus when we look at our feelings, we often edit them in the very moment we look at them. For instance, if we feel fear but either don't want to feel fear or think we should not, then we will upgrade or change that feeling as quickly as we look at it. Shoehorning tries to "force" your true feeling to the surface.

With shoehorning, you pick the basic one-word feeling that seems most accurate at first glance and stick with it for a moment, before you have a chance to make a complex explanation for it. In reality, you are forcing your basic feeling into an overly tight category. If, for instance, you think, "I feel 49% good and 51% angry," then shoehorn your feeling to anger. That doesn't mean you don't feel anything else, it simply means you probably feel more angry than anything else. Once you have identified the fact you have some anger, move on from there to look at why you feel the anger and how you should respond to it.

Emotions are natural responses; they are neither good nor bad. What we do with them, however, is important. If, for instance, you feel sadness or fear, let those emotions run their course. That does not mean if you feel sad you should always remain sad, or if you are angry you should then punish someone. The goal of shoehorning is to identify real feelings and not to bury them before we can deal with them in a healthy way.

11. How do you feel right now in one word? (Use the shoehorn method of good, bad, scared, or angry.)

_____

Describe your feelings as if you had not shoehorned.

_____

_____

_____

_____

Starting with the one key word you got from shoehorning, how would you go on to describe your feelings?

_____

_____

_____

Pick an important event or crisis from your previous week. Think back to that event. What shoehorn word describes it?

    ____ Good   ____ Bad   ____ Scared   ____ Angry

From that word, how would you describe your feelings last week?

_____

_____

_____

SELF-ACCEPTANCE

Acceptance of feelings is very important in recuperation from codependency. Since our faith is built on the decision to trust God instead of our feelings, we need to trust God no matter how we feel. But we should not deny our feelings just because we want to feel another way. How can we cope with the emotional scars from our past if we don't take an honest look at our feelings?

12. Read Philippians 3:9. On what basis can you accept yourself?

_____

_____

Passing On Problems

Perhaps you are a person who has survived a dysfunctional or troubled childhood with an addicted person. Maybe you have been able to identify some of the scars you have brought with you into adulthood. Maybe you are in the process of growing through those difficulties. Nevertheless, there is an additional concern you need to address—how are your scars affecting your own family and friends?

The effects of codependency often cross generational lines. If a child grows up in a home where there was rage and violent outbursts, upon becoming an adult he or she may instinctively or habitually respond in the very same way when encountering stress. Even parents who determine they will treat their own kids completely opposite of the way in which they were treated may have problems. In order to compensate, they may be too tolerant of bad behavior or too lenient in general.

They may also be too strict or controlling. Either way, the effect of the addict's childhood is passed on to the next generation.

✏️ 13. How are behaviors you learned as a child passed on to others in your world?

_____
_____
_____

How do you compensate for childhood experiences in the way you relate to others?

_____
_____
_____

How is God healing you? _____

_____
_____
_____

What scars remain? _____

_____
_____
_____

✏️ 14. Read Isaiah 53:5, Luke 4:18, and Philippians 4:13. What wonderful promise is outlined in these verses?

_____
_____

SUMMARY

Healing from codependency is both important and possible. We do not need to live our lives completely covered by the shadow of dysfunctional people in our lives. God's divine touch will provide a clear picture of where we are in life and what areas of our lives we need to improve.

Let's Review

1. How is God healing the scars of your codependency?

2. What scars remain? How will you deal with them?

3. In 2 Corinthians 13:5, what determines our character under adversity?

4. In step 4 of the "Twelve Steps," what is the litmus test of who we are?

5. Read Lamentations 3:40. List some of our "ways" in the space below, then commit to that promise before God.

STUDY 6

THE BALANCING ACT

We have already looked at some of the common ways people become codependent. But codependency patterns show up in some surprising places! One is in our relationships to groups.

As Christians we are often involved in groups, studies, classes, and programs which are part of the larger church. Hopefully, our motivation for being a part of such social gatherings is not only to find fellowship, but to give fellowship and do ministry, as well as to serve the greater needs of the church.

OVEREXTENSION

While there are never enough laborers in the church, there are usually a dependable few who have a heart to serve at any cost. These faithful workers can easily find themselves facing an "ocean" of need with only a "bucket" of personal resources. Almost every pastor has seen the Christian worker who labors long and hard, becomes overly responsible, suffers burnout or worse—a condition of emotional exhaustion, then falls prey to some old habit or personal problem. Such people have lost touch with themselves—their needs and their limits, losing their identity in various groups of people. If the group does well, they do well; if the group does not, they do not. This pattern of codependency is social codependency.

People who are socially codependent struggle to change groups of people more than they do individuals. But groups, like individuals, are not always ready to change. Without intervention, the social codependent's servant heart can prevent him or her from being the "long distance runner" he or she truly wants to be and the consistent worker the church really needs.

Social codependency can occur outside the church. Here the codependent "lives" to maintain relationships with others. This codependent is wonderful to have around because he or she is so socially oriented. The day comes, however, when the codependent too has nothing more to give, he or she can't maintain all his or her relationships, and falls apart emotionally.

Codependency is not just a matter of dealing with emotional scars from dysfunctional people. Codependency can also reflect our tendency to try to control any of the relationships around us in ways that are not necessarily in accordance with God's will.

1. Read Genesis 4:9. What does it mean to be your "brother's keeper"?

2. Read 2 Thessalonians 3:7-10. What standard of behavior does Paul set forth?

In what areas has God given you responsibility to set an example for other people?

_____
_____
_____
_____
_____

There is a fine line between taking responsibility to set an example, and pushing ourselves beyond healthy limits by being overly responsible.

There are many reasons we may try too hard:
* Fear of displeasing God,
* Making sure we look good in front of others,
* Trying to prevent others from being able to criticize us in any way,
* Compulsive behavior,
* Performing to meet our personal need to be needed.

3. How do you know when you are pushing yourself in a way God does not want you to?

_____
_____
_____
_____

4. In what area of your life are you most likely to be overly responsible?

_____
_____
_____

What do you think your motivation might be? _____

_____
_____
_____

As in other areas of codependent behavior, there is little we can do to address our dysfunctions unless we break through denial and increase our self-awareness. It is important that we clearly know what God wants us to do.

✎ 5. Read 1 Corinthians 12:27-30. What does Paul tell us concerning our role in the body of Christ?

_____
_____
_____
_____

Although each Christian has equal value and importance, there are significant differences in the Church between specific responsibilities, roles, abilities, gifts, and expectations.

Calling

People frequently struggle with the problem of responsibility in the church. Some people try to maintain a role they are not able to fulfill, while others try to achieve a gift or calling that is not really theirs. There are people who try to preach, but really don't have the gift; those who try to heal without either God's timing or calling; and those who try to do administration without the gift to do so.

It is important that we pursue what God wants us to do as opposed to what we prefer to do.

✎ 6. Read Luke 10:41,42. This account of Martha and Mary is an example of ministry touching others' daily needs and responsibilities. Explain how this example applies to our lives today.

_____
_____
_____
_____

What are some areas in which you fulfill responsibilities in order to avoid personal ministry?

_____
_____
_____
_____

THE BALANCING ACT

✏️ 7. In which area(s) of ministry would you prefer to serve?

____ Missions	____ Evangelism	____ Administration
____ Helping	____ Teaching	____ Healing
____ Prophecy	____ Other_____	

Which ministry(ies) do you believe God has called you to?

____ Missions	____ Evangelism	____ Administration
____ Helping	____ Teaching	____ Healing
____ Prophecy	____ Other_____	

In which ministry(ies) do you struggle the most?

____ Missions	____ Evangelism	____ Administration
____ Helping	____ Teaching	____ Healing
____ Prophecy	____ Other_____	

Finding God's Will

✏️ 8. Read John 5:30. In this passage, on what does Jesus indicate we are to focus in our daily struggles?

_____

_____

In this Scripture Jesus not only points out His heart to do God's will, but points out He can do nothing without the Father. This example is important in understanding how to deal with our failures and struggles in doing God's will.

No matter what area we take responsibility in, we cannot succeed without God's strength and guidance. When we stop to think about it—since God never gives us something we cannot handle, we are certain of success in ministry as long as we are doing His will.

✏️ 9. How do you know that the ministry you are doing is God's will for you?

_____

_____

_____

How do you know when you are beginning to depend upon yourself?

_____

_____

_____

Loneliness

10. Read Hebrews 13:5. What promise does God give in this verse?

_____

_____

_____

One of the reasons we get caught in unhealthy relationships is because we are lonely. We jump into relationships and make commitments even when it is unwise to do so.

Loneliness is a common problem, and some people try to blunt its discomfort by being involved in ministry. A great danger in loneliness comes when we are not aware of its influence in our lives. We may find ourselves involved in ministry to meet our emotional needs, rather than to serve God. The result is our effort in ministry is likely to fail or become distorted.

11. Is loneliness an issue in your life? Explain.

_____

_____

_____

Under what circumstances do you feel loneliness the most? (Use shoehorning here.)

_____

_____

_____

_____

There is nothing wrong with using fellowship and even ministry as part of the means of coping with our experiences of loneliness; however, problems will occur if we become dependent upon the ministry or fellowship instead of upon the Lord.

How do you know when you are leaning too heavily on fellowship for dealing with your loneliness?

Only a close, daily relationship with Jesus can truly address loneliness. Mere people can never fulfill our deepest needs.

12. Who can fully comfort the lonely? (See 2 Corinthians 1:3,4.)

_____

_____

Guilt And Shame

Whenever we take an honest look at our flaws and failures, we can easily be overwhelmed by guilt or shame or both. What Christian does not have a "speck" in his or her eye? For example, what Christian has not made the mistake of condemning or judging another person inappropriately, or has failed to love, or has been concerned about personal needs ahead of others? All of our failures can lead to guilt and shame.

Guilt occurs when we feel blame for problems and pain we have had a part in. Shame surfaces when we feel embarrassment for our role in problems and damage in which we have had a part.

Unfortunately, guilt and shame keep us from depending on God, and they keep us from looking at our shortcomings. Yet in order to recover from codependency, it is important to see our failures rather than to cover them up.

13. Read 1 John 1:9. What promise is expressed in this passage of Scripture?

___

God has a wonderful remedy for our failures, and He has peace to offer us in place of our guilt and shame.

14. Read Ephesians 4:32. How does knowing God's forgiveness affect your ability to look at your own failures?

___

SUMMARY

Not only is it important to receive God's forgiveness, but to live in that forgiveness. We need to trust God to change us rather than our own willpower alone. If we try to fix ourselves or compensate for our guilt and shame, we may well disregard forgiveness and begin to operate in our own strength.

LET'S REVIEW

✎ 1. Are there areas in which, or those from whom, you need to ask forgiveness? Refer to Matthew 5:23,24.

_____
_____
_____

✎ 2. Based on James 5:16, what does Christ tell us to do concerning confession of our sins?

_____
_____
_____

✎ 3. Do you need forgiveness for not accepting forgiveness? If so, on the lines below write a prayer asking God to forgive you.

_____
_____
_____
_____
_____

✎ 4. How does 2 Thessalonians 3:7-10 instruct us in Christian behavior?

_____
_____
_____

✎ 5. On whom are we to depend in every situation? (See John 5:30.) Why?

_____
_____
_____

THE BALANCING ACT

STUDY 7

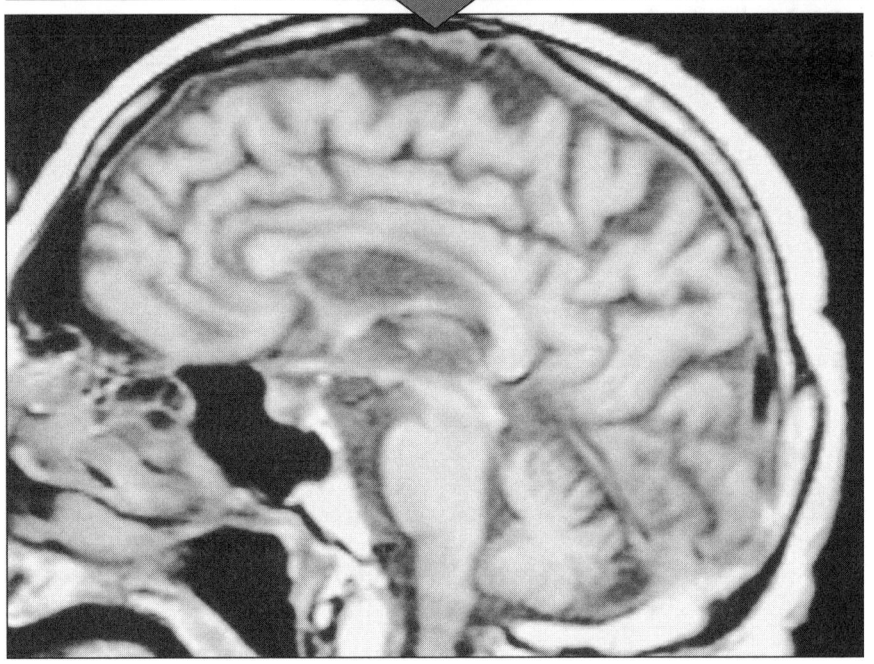

THE BRAIN AND CODEPENDENCY

The tragedy of codependency is reflected in damaged and wasted lives. Codependency exists because we are so easily caught in behaviors we cannot seem to let go of. One of the least understood aspects of such dependent behaviors is *compulsion*.

Everyone has had the experience of making a logical decision to resolve a particular problem, only to find themselves doing quite the opposite. Every person has eaten too much, worked too long, been too controlling, stayed up too late, put off responsibilities despite their best intentions, or experienced some other form of unpreferred behavior. If we are honest, we have never at the end of the day done all we felt we should when we prayed that morning! Our experiences echo the words of Paul in Romans 7:19, in which he expresses his dismay at doing the things he does not want to.

The Chemical Brain

As we have noted in an earlier study, the Scripture makes it perfectly clear even as Christians we are subject to failure. We are like Paul who, despite his best intentions, continued to sin, even though he obviously did not want to. It is through faith that we must rely on God for His deliverance from sin.

The problem of human limitations becomes most obvious in compulsive or dependent behaviors, such as codependency, fear, anger, or anxiety which sometimes seem to run their own course in our lives. We feel anxiety about a situation we just can't seem to shake, no matter how much we pray. We may know intellectually that God has committed himself to keeping us, but we still worry!

Why do we go against our good intentions and better judgment? The problem is our fears, frustrations, anxieties, and dependencies are far more than lack of fortitude. They are not just a matter of inadequate faith. Our limitedness reflects the way in which our bodies, and in particular our nervous system, are put together. It is a limitation we can never completely overcome; a limitedness that, if we understand and accept it, should only drive us to depend more upon God.

If we are to learn to let go and trust God, it is vital to understand how our emotions and bodies work. Unfortunately, emotions are not always easy to manage.

How do emotions work? In overly simple terms, our emotions and behaviors are driven by two dynamics: *brain chemistry* and *brain imprints*.

Brain Chemistry

We are motivated to a great degree by the amount and variation of chemicals in our brains called *neurotransmitters*. These chemicals link activity between each brain cell when we think or experience emotion. People have their own unique chemical "soup" that helps shape their personalities, responses, and ability to cope with stress and emotional pain. Some of these brain chemicals help us with stress, some help us feel "up," some help us with emotional pain, while others calm us down when we need to relax.

Whenever we think thoughts or experience emotion, we utilize our reserves of these specialized chemicals. After an unusually difficult day, for instance, we may well use up too many of the *neurotransmitters* we depend upon to cope with stress. The result is that for the next day or few days, we may experience a lack of motivation or inner strength while our brain chemicals are replenishing.

We often run low on these chemicals just when we have the greatest need of them. Ongoing stress can even use up our chemical reserves without our realizing it. Sometimes, quite by surprise and apparently without reason, we find ourselves less able to deal with stress. Despite our best intentions, some days we are "up," and some days we are "down." We are limited. We cannot simply will ourselves to overcome all of the effects of brain chemical changes. Such changes can easily be misconstrued as failure, lack of faith, some hidden spiritual problem, or even an attitude problem!

Brain Imprints

The second factor that affects our emotional behavior is our *lower brain* (survival). This is the part of our brain that experiences emotions such as stress and trauma. This area has the unique ability to "imprint." That is, the emotional part of our brain becomes sensitized and permanently remembers certain emotional experiences. For instance, if we experienced an abusive situation as a child, and it caused us to develop a fear response, that fear response may stay locked in our *lower brain* our whole lives, returning from time to time despite our best efforts to overcome it with faith, changed behavior, or courage.

It is not uncommon for a codependent who has grown up in abusive situations to feel the impact of those imprinted memories throughout his or her life. Unfortunately, such fears and anxieties only lend themselves to the codependent trying to control relationships even more!

Recovery

Our recovery from codependency must allow for our limited ability to cope with our emotions. We should not think that just because we understand some codependent emotions and responses in our lives we can automatically overcome them. We have to learn to live with our frailty and with the experiences our emotional brains have memorized.

Our recovery must be rooted in God's mercy throughout our lives rather than solely upon our will power and determination to change.

1. Read Psalm 139:1-14. Explain below the significance of this psalm regarding the make-up of a person.

___

___

___

What modern science is just beginning to understand about human behavior is nothing new to our Creator. It is important for us to remember that God knows each of us and all of our limitations personally.

2. When you consider that God knows everything about you, does that make you more secure or less secure? Why?

___

___

___

We have discussed the phenomena of brain chemistry and behavior. Now we will look at a very simple overview of what different brain chemicals do for us.

BRAIN BEHAVIORS

Following is a sampling of neurotransmitters and the effect nervous system chemicals have on human behavior:

Neurochemicals And Codependency

Endorphins—Endorphins (from the Greek "the morphine within") have essentially the same chemical makeup as morphine but are 30 times stronger. They function in our nervous system identically to morphine and produce the same pain-killing and pleasurable effect. Endorphins are the hormones that function in the well-known "runner's high." They even add to the experience of delight when people laugh or are excited, and they comfort us when we cry.

✎ 3. How would you describe the calming effect of endorphins after you have been in an emotional crisis?

___

___

___

How would you describe the pain-killing effect of endorphins after you have been on a long run and have encountered a "second wind"?

___

___

(NE) Norepinephrine—Stress and pain trigger the production of adrenaline and norepinephrine with several profound effects. They raise the body's activity level and strength as well as increase mental concentration and assertiveness. When these are depleted or inadequate, the result is lethargy. By focusing our attention or pushing ourselves emotionally, we cause the release of these chemicals.

✎ 4. What do you do to help yourself feel "ready for action" after you have been relaxing for a while and you need to get busy?

___

___

(5-HT) Serotonin—Serotonin helps us cope with emotional and physical pain. Excess serotonin produces euphoria while insufficient serotonin is associated with both depression and agitation.

(DA) Dopamine—Dopamine affects emotional moods, including those of well-being and euphoria.

(ACH) Acetylcholine—The most prevalent neurotransmitter in the body, acetylcholine plays a crucial role in harmonizing other neurotransmitters. It is also involved in memory functions.

Beyond these dominant transmitters, numerous other brain chemicals affect our experiences of well-being, stress, and emotional pain.

Why is awareness of neurotransmitters so important, especially when we are talking about codependency? Neurotransmitters have a powerful effect on all of our behaviors. For instance, suppose you go through a period of stress such as follows:

Preparing to get married,
Moving,
Worrying constantly about a loved one,

Being constantly bitter,
Dealing with a great emotional crisis,
Physical illness.

The result of any of the above experiences may be the depletion of your central nervous system (brain) of the chemicals it needs to cope with stress. The reaction to this depletion may be one or more of the following:

Tiredness,
Reduced ability to cope with stress,
Less positive attitude,
Increased sensitivity to emotional and physical pain,
Increased vulnerability to certain illnesses,
Headaches.

(All of the above symptoms vary according to the degree and length of stress and the condition and especially the age of the person experiencing stress.)

5. Can you recall a recent negative stressful period in your life that was followed by a few days of feeling less resilient than normal? What happened?

_____

_____

_____

Can you recall a recent positive stressful period (such as a busy vacation) in your life that was followed by a few days of feeling less resilient than normal? What happened?

_____

_____

_____

The experience of neurochemical depletion is one of vague discomfort and vulnerability. We instinctively know something is wrong, but our awareness of what we are experiencing may be so slight it may never occur to us that we are going through the physical/emotional letdown of neurotransmitter depletion.

Neurotransmitter depletion would not be such a big issue, except many compulsive people, such as addicts and codependents, have developed a dysfunctional system to overcome depletion. They do so not with patience and rest but by driving themselves harder! When they become depleted, they tend to push themselves harder in order to release their few remaining neurochemicals. As a result, they may feel better temporarily, only to feel worse later when they are even lower on neurochemicals. This response pattern may even become a habit where they continue to push themselves in order to feel normal inside, yet never allow their neurochemical resources to really replenish themselves. In fact they can become addicted to the abuse of their own neurotransmitters.

✎ 6. Have you ever found that you pushed yourself too long or too hard to the point it became habit to push yourself? Explain.

___

___

___

___

Trying to "fix" our neurochemical imbalances, that is, trying to feel better by the use or abuse of such antidotes as food or caffeine, is a common result of chronic neurochemical depletion. Other common methods include overworking and running too fast emotionally.

Fixing neurodepletion by trying harder or going faster rather than facing natural limits is precisely what causes the progressive cycle of addiction to occur; that is, more effort for less result to feeling worse to more effort for less result.

✎ 7. Have you ever noticed yourself pushing hard just to keep going? What happened?

___

___

___

Have you ever found yourself too tired to slow down? What did it feel like?

___

___

___

The cycle of addiction by depletion is most evident in the case of codependency. The codependent's desperate efforts to maintain a dysfunctional relationship only drag them in deeper. The more they try to fix the relationship, the more tired they get, until they are running on empty, unable to function normally and unable to stop.

✎ 8. If you have been in a codependent relationship(s), what happened in it when you completely ran out of energy?

___

___

___

✎ 9. One of the most stressful experiences in life is to live in a codependent relationship. If you have been in a dysfunctional relationship(s), how did your experience with that relationship feel after you were deeply involved in it?

_____

_____

_____

✎ 10. Read James 1:23,24. How are we to view ourselves based on this portion of Scripture?

_____

_____

_____

Self-Awareness And Acceptance

In the light of God's Word, there is no way we can effectively cope with dependent or addictive behaviors unless we understand them for what they are.

For instance, if we have codependent behaviors (and such behaviors are common), then we have a dependency; if we have a dependency, we have an addiction.

Why is identifying addictive behavior important? Simply this: addictive behavior is behavior beyond our control and points us to our need of God's intervention.

Admitting we lack control is not to say we have justification for failed character; it does mean we cannot do everything perfectly or right. We cannot control all of our behaviors. We can control some of our behaviors all the time, some of our behaviors some of the time, and some of our behaviors none of the time. The woman, for instance, who keeps a perfect house and controls her diet so as not to gain an ounce of extra weight may not have time to fulfill God's laws about sacrificial living. The rage alcoholic who can keep perfect control until circumstances become too stressful also eventually falls. No one is perfect.

If we are persuaded that we can by focus or motivation correct and control all of our behaviors, then either we are in denial or we have no character flaws whatsoever, and in turn, no dependency or addictions. But if we do indeed have addictive behavior we need to see it not as something we can fix alone, but something that God needs to help us change.

✎ 11. Over what do you feel you have the most control? Why?

_____

_____

Over what do you feel you have the least control? Why? _____

_____

How would the answers you have just given change if you were suddenly injured in an accident and permanently hospitalized?

_____

_____

_____

✎ 12. Read Psalm 103:13-18. What does this passage tell us of our human frailty?

_____

_____

_____

Being Truthful With Our Strengths And Weaknesses

In Psalm 103, David reminds us of our frail situation as humans. We need to remember our frailty.

Some people think that by sheer motivation they can overcome neurochemical depletion, but they couldn't be more wrong. The strongest, most motivated person in the world simply cannot perform past the limits of his or her own neurochemical system. When there are no neurochemical resources left, the toughest fighter in all the world will simply give up and wait for the end.

✎ 13. How do you know when you are reaching the end of your neurochemical resources?

_____

_____

_____

✎ 14. Read 1 Corinthians 12:18-20. What does this tell us about the way we interact with each other?

_____

_____

_____

Genetic/Behavioral Differences

One of the things that makes us different from one another is found in the subtle differences of our bio-chemical makeup. Each of us has differing amounts of such neurochemicals as norepinephrine. The result is that some of us are consistently more "up" than others and may have a higher tolerance for stress.

✎ 15. First Corinthians 12:18 states that God created each of us different from one another. Based on this, answer the following questions:

When you compare yourself to other people, how do you see your natural resilience to stress?

_____

Has God made you more an "up" person or a "down" person? _____

Do you have dreams of completely changing who you are? Are those changes what God wants or only what you desire? Explain.

_____

_____

_____

Forgiveness

Know that God wants us to understand our personal limitations and recognize limitations in others, and in that, exercise forgiveness for yourself and toward other people. We need to realize our help in this awareness and forgiveness process is a total dependence upon God! Jesus teaches us it is essential to forgive.

✎ 16. Read Mark 11:25. What does this passage tell us about forgiveness?

_____

_____

How does understanding your limitations help you forgive others? _____

_____

_____

How does understanding your limitations help you accept forgiveness for yourself?

_____

_____

SUMMARY

It is important to recognize the part chemical balance plays in human experience. Identifying the early signs of chemical depletion and acting appropriately will help those who are trapped in chemical-induced despair free themselves. This cycle of dependency is best broken by leaning on the strength of Christ.

Let's Review

✎ 1. How do brain imprints impact a person's life?

✎ 2. What is a neurotransmitter?

✎ 3. What is the result of depletion of neurotransmitters?

✎ 4. How can neurotransmitters be restored?

✎ 5. How can depletion of neurotransmitters destroy those who have addictive personalities?

STUDY 8

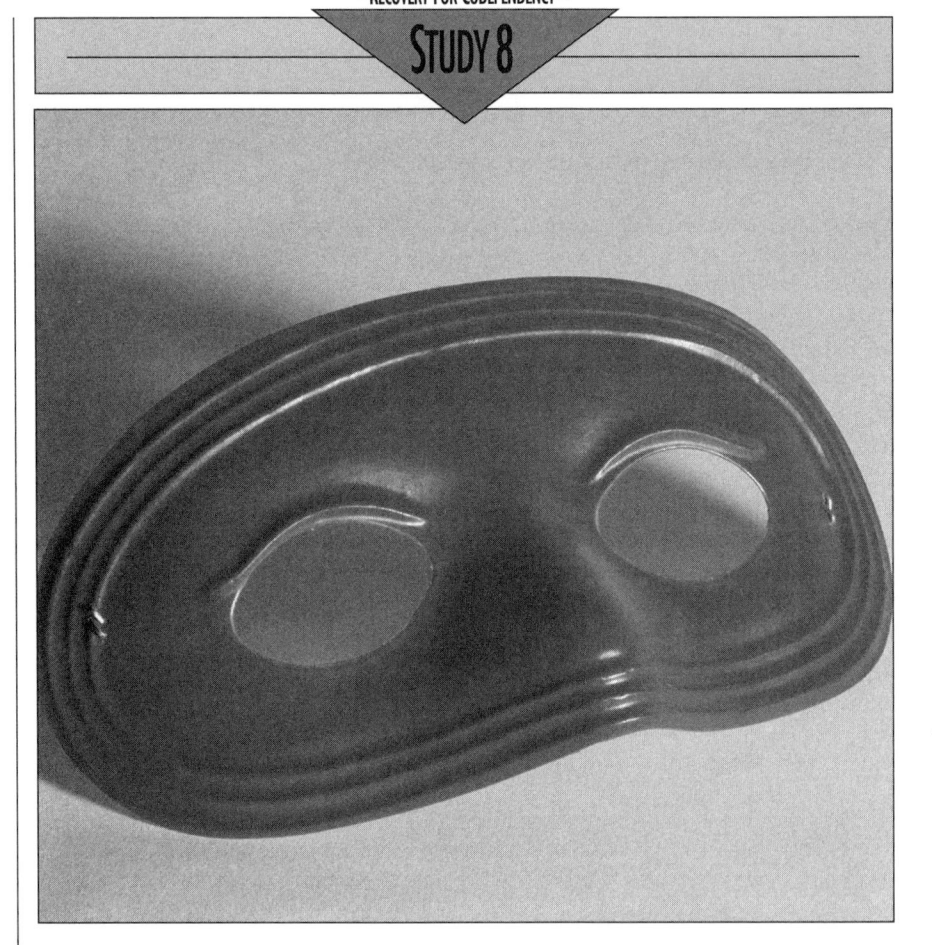

MYTHS OF CODEPENDENCY

There is a lot of day-to-day advice you may hear about dealing with codependency that may not be true! In this study we will look at several principles related to codependency that can help us separate fact from fiction.

Has anyone ever told you, "You have to take care of yourself before you can really help others!" It is advice that sounds good, but it is not necessarily true for the Christian. Firstly, whatever we are able to offer to help other people comes from God and not from us anyway; secondly, if we try to fix ourselves before we help others or do ministry, we may never get around to doing it.

LOVE YOURSELF FIRST

There are times when God asks us to give and serve well beyond our emotional resources; to give sacrificially. The Bible tells us we are to die to ourselves and live to God (2 Corinthians 5:15). The challenge of recovery then, is for us to spend ourselves in the way God wants us to. We should avoid burning ourselves out doing ministry that is conceived more in our intention to do good than in the heart of God. We should not be trying harder to help someone than they are trying themselves. However, we should not hesitate to spend ourselves for God; He will be our strength.

1. Read 1 Corinthians 10:24. What does Paul instruct us to do in this Scripture passage?

___

How do you personally know when sacrifice for others is appropriate?

___

2. Read 2 Corinthians 12:14-20. Is Paul being codependent? Explain.

___

Don't Do For Others What They Can Do For Themselves

Perhaps someone has told you, "If you help that person by taking some of their responsibility, you're just being a 'crutch' to them." That principle may be true at times. There are instances where taking the load off someone's shoulders keeps them from growing and may even harm them. But there are also times where it may save their lives! How do you know the difference? By doing what God tells you to do.

3. Record an experience where you helped someone when they really could not help themselves.

___

Codependency: Not The Same For Everyone

Some cultures put less priority on individualism and put more focus on nuclear or extended families. Everyone is expected to sacrifice individuality for each other. This pattern of living is not unhealthy, it is just different. What is codependency for one person may not be for another.

Codependency can still occur in cultures that share more in common. In any culture people can trust too much in anything other than God and try to control their own lives.

✎ 4. How does your cultural background affect your tendency toward codependency?

✎ 5. How does your family background affect your tendency toward codependency?

Self-Esteem: The Cure For Codependency?

How many times have you heard that self-esteem is critical to our personal development? The Scripture has its own interesting perspective on esteem.

✎ 6. Read Romans 12:3. Explain Paul's instruction to us concerning self-esteem.

In the 12th chapter of Romans, Paul gives us instruction about perceiving ourselves in honest and realistic terms.

We live in a world where we are constantly bombarded with the idea of "self-esteem." Many assume if we have high self-esteem, we will be less likely to pursue self-destructive behaviors; if we like ourselves, we will be less likely to overeat, use drugs, or be dysfunctional.

One reason for this perception is people who have addictions and other dysfunctions are often quick to talk about themselves in negative terms—"I'm not worth anything," "No one cares about me," "I don't want to try anymore," etc. They may allow themselves to be trampled on. The assumption is if such people have high self-esteem, they will take care of themselves and avoid or overcome dysfunctional and addictive behavior.

There are two problems with this assumption. The first problem is that much addictive behavior can't be controlled by willpower; addictive behavior can't be corrected by just trying harder. Again, depletion of neurochemicals associated with addiction is worsened by strenuous efforts to quit. This depletion in turn causes "imprints" to awaken and relapse to occur. It is hard to find a person with an addiction that does not want to correct his or her problem. Often the person has tried rigorously and frequently to break free of the addiction, or at least control its progression, for years.

Some addicts will say they don't care, but that is usually because they have simply given up trying. Since they know that one more try will probably bring more failure, they ease their dismay by saying they don't care. But the truth is if they could find an easy solution to their addiction, they would grab it without hesitation. People act like they don't care about themselves because of hopelessness, not low self-esteem.

The second problem with the assumption that high self-esteem can solve addictions is an ironic one. Addictive behavior breeds survival instincts and focus on self. The fact is, people with almost any kind of serious problem tend to think about their own difficulties first, and anyone else's troubles a distinct second. Depressed, addicted, and codependent people will often talk exhaustively about their dilemmas. In fact, their whole world seems to revolve around themselves. Yet they will refer to themselves and their circumstances in such negative terms it appears they have no self-esteem.

The result of focusing excessively on our own problems leads us to think primarily of ourselves. In reality, by putting ourselves first we esteem ourselves very highly!

In the recovery community, such self-focus is sometimes referred to as "terminal uniqueness"—the idea that no one else has trouble like you do. Such self-focusing often leads to self-pity, self-pity in turn leads to blame, and blame returns to codependency.

The Scriptures tell us the way out of this dilemma—we must give up our lives to save them, and honor others more than ourselves (Matthew 10:39; Romans 12:10). This letting go of self is a quicker road to freedom than endless attempts at self-repair. God is always ready to make us over completely.

7. Read Ephesians 5:2 and 1 John 3:1,16. Does God have high esteem for you? How do you know?

_____

_____

Are you aware when you are experiencing self-pity? How do you cope with it?

_____

_____

_____

8. Read Luke 6:31. Do you esteem others as much as you would like them to esteem you?

_____

_____

Can you love others as much as yourself without God's help? Explain.

_____
_____

✎ 9. Read Mark 12:31 and Romans 13:8. Explain the differences between God's love and human love.

_____
_____
_____

How do you feel about yourself when you love others in a healthy way?

_____
_____

Did God put the ability for healthy love in you or did you just discover it? Explain.

_____
_____

GUARD AGAINST RELAPSE

✎ 10. Read 2 Timothy 2:11-19. What trustworthy saying is Paul giving us here? What effect does this have on our relationship with God?

_____
_____
_____

How do you feel when you know you have failed God?

_____
_____

How do you come to know that God still loves you after you fail?

_____
_____

Losing ground or experiencing a relapse is a threat with any addictive or dependent behavior. Relapse is obvious in the case of a recovering alcoholic who goes on a binge, or a heroin user who once again injects heroin. In the case of codependency, however, relapse may be far less obvious and is often more frequent. Why? Because it is so easy to slip into control relationships.

11. Does codependent behavior happen frequently in your life? Explain.

_____

_____

_____

_____

What constitutes relapse in codependency? Definitions vary, but it could be argued that relapse occurs anytime we begin to once again control people, places, or things in a way that is not in the will of God.

Path Of Relapse

* Allowing someone to constantly manipulate you.
* Trying to fix another person's problem when he or she doesn't want to change.
* Being stressed about someone else's decisions or lifestyle.
* Blaming others for the difficulty in your life.
* Denying your feelings when you should express them.
* Trying to control events in your life to insure personal comfort and security whether or not God wants you to control them.

When you consider relapse in these terms, it is easy to see how the codependent can be prone to chronic relapse.

Of course there are those who may say, "I don't have that type of (codependent) relationship anymore." This may be quite an assumption. No matter how you frame it, frequent relapse in codependency is all too easy.

Signs Of Relapse

Defensiveness	Anger
Compulsiveness	Irregular eating
Impulsiveness	Lack of motivation
"Tunnel" vision and hearing	Stress disorders
Depression	Rejection of help
Repeated failed plans	The "I don't care" response
Little constructive planning	Dissatisfaction with life
Giving up	Self-pity
Idle daydreams-fantasy, romance	Lying/dishonesty to control situations
Immature desire to be happy	Loss of self-confidence
Confusion	Resentments
Irritation with friends	Loneliness and tension/isolation

✏️ 12. List the signs of relapse you think you would have a tendency to fall into if you returned to codependency.

_____
_____
_____
_____

Which signs would be hardest for you to identify?

_____
_____

Myths Of Relapse

* **Myth:** Relapse always has a warning.
* **Fact:** Our tendency to relapse may come with or without a warning.

* **Myth:** Having no codependent relationship means you are in recovery.
* **Fact:** Abstinence is not necessarily recovery. Recovery is the condition of coping with addictions or dysfunctional behavior through God's mercy rather than our own strength. You can abstain from any kind of addiction for a season without really depending on God.

* **Myth:** Once you are aware of relapse, you can choose to take action against it.
* **Fact:** Just because you are aware you are making a mistake doesn't always mean you are able to reverse it. Sometimes God has to intervene.

* **Myth:** Relapse can be avoided by willpower and discipline.
* **Fact:** Personal effort alone rarely saves anyone from acute addiction or dependency.

* **Myth:** People who relapse are not motivated to recover.
* **Fact:** Just because we make mistakes doesn't mean we don't want to do better.

✏️ 13. Which myth has had the most impact on you?

_____
_____
_____
_____

Sacrificial Service

✎ 14. Read Luke 6:31-35. To whom are we to exhibit God's love? Why?

_____

_____

_____

Sadly, in a well-meaning effort to fulfill these words of Jesus, some Christians have poured heart and soul into a relationship with an addict or dysfunctional person, only to find themselves caught in a codependent relationship.

As a result of some of these catastrophes, many people who don't have a clear understanding of either codependency or recovery have determined to never again get involved in unfamiliar relationships and never to sacrifice too much. You may hear conversations in which one person declines to help another because they don't want to be codependent. Someone might say, "I don't want to help that person because that could develop into an unhealthy attitude of reliance!"

Such responses entirely miss the point of recovery from codependency. Scriptural instructions to care for those in need and to love one another still stand. But so do scriptural instructions to follow God's will. Jesus not only comforted the afflicted; He challenged the comfortable. He did not waste time helping those who did not want help, yet He did not hesitate helping those who wanted to change. In every point He did what God wanted rather than ministering at random.

We too must do exactly as God leads us. We must help and sacrifice for others as God instructs and leads us. In so doing we will avoid trying to run other people's lives or foolishly trying to rescue them. In short, we will be able to minister without becoming codependent.

✎ 15. How have you done ministry outside of God's will? What happened as a result?

_____

_____

_____

Have you turned away service opportunity knowing it was God's will? Why?

_____

_____

✎ 16. Read Matthew 12:50. How does Jesus describe our role in the family of God?

_____

_____

We have family responsibility with all Christians. That is a lot of responsibility!

✎ 17. How does doing the will of God affect your relationship with Christians in need?

_____

_____

_____

How does doing the will of God affect your relationship with non-Christians in need?

_____

_____

_____

How do you tell someone you love "no" without hurting or manipulating them?

_____

_____

_____

✎ 18. Read Hebrews 10:22. What does the writer of Hebrews encourage us to do?

_____

_____

When we try to get other people to change their behavior in order to serve God, that activity may become codependent if we:
* Try to force change in our own strength and time,
* Presume the outcome of our efforts,
* Try to control the outcome of an effort,
* Become more involved than we are supposed to,
* Become less involved than we are supposed to.

SUMMARY

Let us purpose to resolve the mistakes we have made when associated with a codependent relationship. Further, let us be challenged to greater spiritual growth and responsibility as we learn to place complete trust in God while seeking His will in everything we do. In all of this we are to honor others in the same way God would and reach out to them in love and good works.

LET'S REVIEW

✎ 1. What is the most important ministry God has given you? How do you know this?

✎ 2. How well do you turn ministry over after you have done what you are supposed to do?

✎ 3. What does Romans 12:3 indicate concerning our self-esteem?

✎ 4. Explain the difference between God's love and human love (Mark 12:31 and Romans 13:8).

✎ 5. In Matthew 12:50, what is the Christian's responsibility?

• RECOVERY FOR CODEPENDENCY •

STUDY 9

THE FINAL STEPS

So far we have focused on problems uniquely related to codependency. Now we will look at the scriptural pattern of recovery, specifically how to live our lives in order to cope with dysfunctional behaviors. We will also complete our journey through the *Twelve Steps* as it relates to Scripture.

The term *recovery* is used by millions of people around the world to explain the phenomenon of escape from addiction. The term is so popular it has come to mean different things to different people. For some, recovery simply means sobriety. For many, recovery means salvation as Christians understand from the Scripture. For others, it means the ability to finally control addiction. The most common understanding of recovery, however, is just the opposite of having control; it is surrendering control of our lives and depending on God for survival.

RECOVERY FOR THE CODEPENDENT

We will use the term *recovery* to describe the saving help of God from compulsive behaviors, whether those behaviors are drug or alcohol dependency, overeating, controlling behavior, codependency, or any other life-affecting struggle. Recovery is to depend on God where we cannot depend on ourselves.

1. When you first heard the term *recovery*, what did you assume it to mean?

_____
_____
_____
_____

2. How would you define *recovery* now?

_____
_____
_____
_____

3. Read Philippians 3:8-11. Explain Paul's motivation in this passage.

_____
_____
_____

Paul's image of trusting in Christ is a good reflection of what recovery commonly means to Christians in the Twelve Step or recovery community.

In summary, recovery is:

* Communion - Walking in close relationship with God, depending on Him to help us.

* Submission - Turning our wills over to God so we make the choices He wants in our lives instead of our own choices.

* Powerlessness - Constant awareness of our frailty and vulnerability. Instead of relying on our own strength to avoid compulsive behaviors, we rely on God's strength.

* Humility - With God's help, maintaining an acute awareness of our own continued shortcomings so our experience of righteousness comes from the Cross, rather than our personal efforts of spiritual achievement.

Codependency is not a dysfunction we overcome just because we become aware of it, any more than we overcome all of our other shortcomings just because we know they exist. God needs to help us with codependency day by day or we will continue to lose ground. Recovery from codependency is rarely a smooth road because unlike the case with alcohol or drug addictions where we can avoid drugs of choice, we often must remain in the very relationships from which we need to recover.

As long as we are in relationships we will make mistakes. As long as it is possible to fall prey to the temptation of controlling others or conversely allowing ourselves to be controlled when we should not, we will occasionally lose sight of our recovery. So how is it possible to find our own way through the myriad of relationships and responsibilities we encounter in life without, on occasion, slipping into codependency? The answer lies only in yielding to God, in communion with the Good Shepherd. We will never live perfectly, but no matter how we do, the Good Shepherd constantly will guide us back onto the path of righteousness if we trust Him and maintain close relationship with Him so we can receive His direction.

4. Read John 15:4. According to this passage, to whom should we offer our affections?

___

Communion

In the parable of the vine and the branches, Jesus clearly instructs us we cannot function effectively in His kingdom without remaining in fellowship with Him. In order for good to come from our lives, God must be our source in all things.

One of the most important dynamics of recovery is communion; fellowship with our Creator. Recovery from codependency is not something we create or attain to. It is a gift, pure and simple. It is a gift we must embrace.

5. When you feel caught in personal shortcomings, does that failure lead you closer to God or make you feel more distant?

___

How do you experience God as your source?

___

6. Read 1 Thessalonians 5:17; 2 Timothy 3:16,17; Hebrews 10:25; 2 Peter 1:19; and 1 John 2:3. What four things can we do to commune with God?

___

✏️ 7. Read Hebrews 12:2. According to the writer of Hebrews, where is our focus to be?

_____

Trust

The writer of Hebrews reminds us our faith is founded upon our relationship with Jesus, the Good Shepherd. It is not our circumstance: the people around us, the places we have to live, or the things that happen to us which seem to either make or destroy our lives. Our security is in God, and it is God's mercy which makes a way for us.

One of the experiences typically associated with addiction of any sort is the tendency to struggle with or try to overly control people, places, or things:

* People - Keeping the relationships in our life in the most secure and comfortable order. The desire to fix or control relationships, of course, lends itself to codependency.

* Places - Staying away from places that have difficult experiences associated with them, and trying to control our environment to make ourselves feel the most comfortable and secure.

* Things - Trying to control things such as houses, cars, finances, or employment in order to make ourselves feel secure.

We all have responsibilities to take care of ourselves and others, but we must do so under the direction of God. While control plays a necessary role in our lives, it is easy to grab control and forget to trust God with the people, places, and things in our lives.

✏️ 8. Describe your struggle or success with each of the following areas of your life.

People: _____

_____

_____

Places: _____

_____

_____

Things: _____

_____

_____

Honest Self-Inventory

In the process of recovery, it is important to go beyond a one-time look at our limits and frailty. We need to remain aware of our limitations if we are to continue to hunger for God's righteousness.

✏️ 9. List your greatest strengths and weaknesses on the lines below. (If a strength or weakness is too private or personal to put on paper, then simply commit it to memory.)

Strengths	Weaknesses

Which of the above areas is God helping you work on currently? How so?

Which area is the hardest to work on? Why?

Gratitude

✏️ 10. Read Psalm 23:1-6 and John 10:11. Explain the implications of this passage to Christians.

In these Scriptures, Jesus presents himself as the Good Shepherd. Not only has He taken care of us, but He always will. Recovery is all about trusting the Good Shepherd to lead us into a life of recovery. If indeed we trust the Good Shepherd, He will lead us to victory.

Sometimes God led King David by still waters, but sometimes David was led through the Valley of the Shadow of Death. God brought him to both places. By logic then, if David is to be thankful for the leading of the Shepherd, he must be grateful no matter where he is led. Such gratitude is essential or we will find ourselves wanting to go other places than where the Shepherd leads us.

We need to live as the popular saying goes—in an "attitude of gratitude."

✎ 11. For what things are you most grateful?

_____
_____
_____

What difficult things in your life are you most grateful for and why? _____

_____
_____
_____

✎ 12. According to 2 Corinthians 12:7-10, how does God use circumstances for our good?

_____
_____
_____

God can take the bad things in our lives and use them to make us better people. He can use our recovery from codependency to draw us closer to Him. How have you drawn closer to God in your recovery?

✎ 13. Read James 1:19-25. What can obeying the moral law do for the Christian?

_____
_____
_____
_____

WORKING THE STEPS

James talks about the dilemma of looking in a mirror only to then forget what you look like. It is a reminder to us that simply reading or studying something without experiencing change is a waste of time.

Doing something about codependency is certainly as important as reading about it or studying it. The Twelve Steps are a wonderful way to get started.

Perhaps the idea of working the Scripture-based Twelve Steps is as new to you as the idea of recovery. You may wonder if you really need to "work" the steps. (In fact, many people who first look at the steps think, *I knew that*, or *That's nothing new*.)

Whether you understand the theory of the steps or not, working them is important in coping with addiction. It is not enough to just be aware of the steps.

14. What steps are you taking to get help for problem areas in your life?

_____

_____

_____

_____

Which of the Twelve Steps seems the hardest to you and why?

_____

_____

_____

_____

It is important to get some help from someone else who has already worked their way through the steps! If you are a church-going Christian with an addiction problem such as codependency—get some help. With some problems, failing to ask for help can prove quite costly.

"Wait," you may say. "Why don't I just pray about my problem instead of going for outside help?" Of course you should pray! But while you are praying, ask God to show you if He has provided outside help for you.

Where are some places you may find help? Start by looking around your church. If you don't find help in the church from someone who understands your problem, don't give up on your church. Go to any kind of Twelve Step meeting in your community and ask a Christian in recovery to "sponsor" you. He or she will help you get started in working your way through the steps, and give you support in learning to trust God with your personal struggles such as codependency.

The Twelve Steps have been used for decades to help change the lives of those with addictive behavior. But one of the biggest surprises about the steps is they barely address drugs or addictive behavior. What they do address are basic scriptural principles for change. As Christians we should automatically be, as they say, in the recovery community, "working the steps," all the time.

✎ 15. Read Psalm 119:105. Where does this passage direct us in our effort?

_____

When you work the Twelve Steps, read the scriptural contexts from which they came, for the Bible is the true light for your path.

✎ 16. Write down some Scriptures that are an encouragement to you. (If you don't remember the reference or exact wording, write down the primary idea.)

_____
_____
_____
_____
_____

To which step does this principle relate most closely?

_____
_____
_____

Which of the Twelve Steps in this study series has had the most impact on you? Why?

_____
_____
_____
_____

SUMMARY

The two Great Commandments set the pattern for our lives and our recovery.

It is important to remember that recovery is ultimately not for ourselves. It is for God's purpose; it is so that He can use us to help other people. All too often, as people ponder their dysfunctions, they begin to think of recovery as a means of only helping themselves. In reality it is a means of serving God, for as we lose our lives, we find them again.

LET'S REVIEW

1. According to Philippians 3:8-11, what motivated Paul? In what way?

2. Read Hebrews 12:2. What does our faith hinge on? Why?

3. List some of your weaknesses that have been turned into strengths.

4. What comfort do the following Scriptures provide? (Psalm 23:1-6 and John 10:11)

5. How can God use your recovery to help other people?

SPIRITUAL DISCOVERY SERIES

Interested in other titles? The *Spiritual Discovery Series* will consist of 40 titles when completed, covering 4 broad categories: Foundations, Life Issues, Biblical Book Studies, and Critical Concerns. All aspects of the series are designed to encourage interaction between the user and the biblical text to enhance internalization of biblical truths. The next few pages give a partial listing of the *Spiritual Discovery Series*, with very brief descriptions.

A New Way Of Life by Robert L. Brandt introduces new converts to the major practices and beliefs of the Pentecostal/Charismatic community. The biblical basis of various doctrines are discussed.
Study Guide 02-0104 **Leader's Guide** 02-0204

Spiritual Devotion by Dr. Nathan H. Nelson explores the art and discipline of developing one's spiritual relationship to God. This study challenges individuals to go beyond mechanical devotional routine toward intimacy with God.
Study Guide 02-0107 **Leader's Guide** 02-0207

Baptized In The Spirit by Frank M. Boyd will help learners understand the nature of the Holy Spirit, His ministry, the biblical basis for the baptism in the Holy Spirit, the initial evidence, and more.
Study Guide 02-0111 **Leader's Guide** 02-0211

A Heart For The Lost by Robert L. Brandt will motivate individuals to prepare themselves for the task of evangelizing. It explores the basis of evangelism and proposes a biblical standard for performing the task.
Study Guide 02-0113 **Leader's Guide** 02-0213

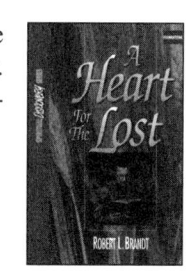

Biblical Foundations by Donald F. Johns explores 13 commonly held Pentecostal beliefs and leads the learner into an understanding of the biblical basis for each. Topics include salvation, water baptism, and the baptism in the Holy Spirit.
Study Guide 02-0118 **Leader's Guide** 02-0218

Living By The Spirit by Lorraine Mastrorio introduces readers to the Spirit baptism experience, describes the fruit of the Spirit, and encourages them to allow God to use them through the supernatural and ministry gifts. It provides direction for Pentecostal believers in their quest to live a Spirit-led lifestyle.
Study Guide 02-0123 **Leader's Guide** 02-0223

Parenting The Elementary Child by Dr. Raymond T. Brock addresses developmental stages, discipline techniques, developing a spiritual climate in the home, financial stress, and intimacy challenges faced during this time.
Study Guide 02-0109 **Leader's Guide** 02-0209

Parenting: The Early Years by Kay E. Marchand is designed to address issues confronted by new parents—prenatal through preschool. Various aspects of parenting are explored, including introducing a child to Jesus.
Study Guide 02-0106 **Leader's Guide** 02-0206

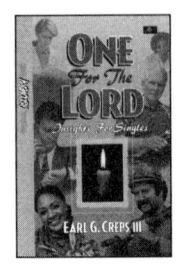

One For The Lord by Dr. Earl G. Creps helps singles examine their position in the world, their place in the Church, and their relationship to God. Learners will be encouraged to discover God's purpose and fulfillment in their lives.
Study Guide 02-0117 **Leader's Guide** 02-0217

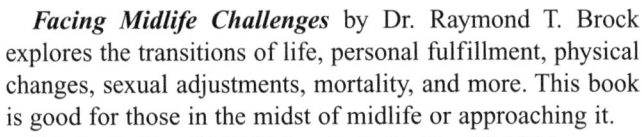

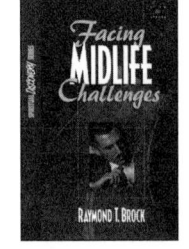

Facing Midlife Challenges by Dr. Raymond T. Brock explores the transitions of life, personal fulfillment, physical changes, sexual adjustments, mortality, and more. This book is good for those in the midst of midlife or approaching it.
Study Guide 02-0115 **Leader's Guide** 02-0215

How To Study The Bible by G. Raymond Carlson introduces the learner to the background of our present Bible, rationale for studying the biblical text, and techniques to enrich the believer's Bible study experience.
Study Guide 02-0108 **Leader's Guide** 02-0208

Bible Prophecy by Dr. Stanley M. Horton will help learners discover the purpose of prophecy, methods of interpretation, and specific events which the Bible clearly predicts.
Study Guide 02-0105 **Leader's Guide** 02-0205

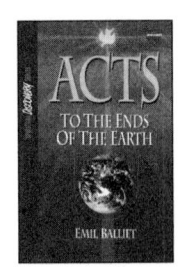

Acts: To The Ends Of The Earth by Emil Balliet is an inductive study that helps the learner understand the historical context and theological content of the Book of Acts, highlighting the eternal principles introduced by the Holy Spirit.
Study Guide 02-0112 **Leader's Guide** 02-0212

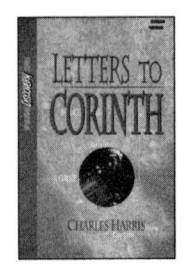

Letters To Corinth by Dr. Charles Harris engages the learner in an inductive examination of the letters of 1 and 2 Corinthians. This study provides answers to various issues faced by local churches throughout history. Users will find fulfillment as they learn to offer themselves in service to others.
Study Guide 02-0116 **Leader's Guide** 02-0216

Romans by G. Raymond Carlson examines Paul's letter to the Romans introducing learners to many of the theological concepts vital to the Christian experience such as original sin, sanctification, justification, Redemption, and the Atonement.
Study Guide   02-0119 **Leader's Guide**   02-0219

Letters From Prison by Lauren W. Orchard examines Paul's letters to the churches of Ephesus, Colosse, and Philippi and to Philemon. It shares God's design for a personal relationship with God and with those whom believers fellowship.
Study Guide   02-0121 **Leader's Guide**   02-0221

Sanctity Of Life by Michael H. Clarensau focuses on the biblical perspective on life issues facing today's Church. Issues examined include the power of death, abortion, genetic engineering, suicide, murder, genocide, and euthanasia.
Study Guide   02-0110 **Leader's Guide**   02-0210

Combating The Darkness by John T. Maempa will help believers recognize and respond appropriately to spiritual attacks. Maempa directs the learner to a firm foundation of biblical passages on which to stand strong in warfare.
Study Guide   02-0114 **Leader's Guide**   02-0214

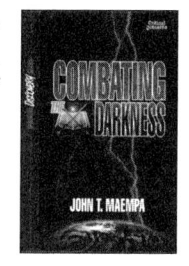

Journey To Integrity by Michael H. Clarensau proclaims the importance of character in the Christian's life. Clarensau recognizes integrity is a process and provides a plan which, if followed, will lead to the user's desired destination.
Study Guide   02-0120 **Leader's Guide**   02-0220

The ***Spiritual Discovery Series*** can be used by individuals in a personal Bible study setting, in a home fellowship group, mid-week service, or in the Sunday School classroom. A *Leader's Guide* is available for those wishing to use this series in a group setting. It includes the *Study Guide* text, methodology to guide group sessions, and reproducible resource items to reinforce the study theme.

Additional titles in the ***Spiritual Discovery Series*** are projected to be released through the summer of 2000. Please contact your *Radiant Life* supplier or see your *Radiant Life* order form if you are interested in any of the books described here or have questions about other titles that might be available.

—*SDS* Staff